JOHN FIELD
AND THE
NOCTURNE

JOHN FIELD AND THE NOCTURNE

Allan J. Wagenheim

Copyright © 2006 by Allan J. Wagenheim.
Second Printing, June 2008

Library of Congress Number: 2005909379
ISBN: Softcover   978-1-4257-0019-5

All rights reserved. No part of this book may be reproduced or transmitted in any form or by any means, electronic or mechanical, including photocopying, recording, or by any information storage and retrieval system, without permission in writing from the copyright owner.

This book was printed in the United States of America.

To order additional copies of this book, contact:
Xlibris Corporation
1-888-795-4274
www.Xlibris.com
Orders@Xlibris.com
31259

CONTENTS

Acknowledgements 9

Chapter One: In the Beginning 11
Chapter Two: John Field and Franz Liszt 16
Chapter Three: John Field, F.J. Haydn, and W.A. Mozart 20
Chapter Four: John Field and L. van Beethoven 27
Chapter Five: Nocturne No. 1 34
Chapter Six: Nocturne No. 2 43
Chapter Seven: Nocturne No. 3 48
Chapter Eight: Nocturne No. 4 55
Chapter Nine: Nocturne No. 5 61
Chapter Ten: Nocturne No. 6 65
Chapter Eleven: Nocturne No. 7 71
Chapter Twelve: Nocturne No. 8 76
Chapter Thirteen: Nocturne No. 9 81
Chapter Fourteen: Nocturne No. 10 86
Chapter Fifteen: Nocturne No. 11 94
Chapter Sixteen: Nocturne No. 12 102
Chapter Seventeen: Nocturne No. 13 103
Chapter Eighteen: Nocturne No. 14 108
Chapter Nineteen: Nocturne No. 15 112
Chapter Twenty: Nocturne No. 16 118
Chapter Twenty-One: Nocturne No. 17 126
Chapter Twenty-Two: Nocturne No. 18 128
Chapter Twenty-Three: The Enigmatic Genius 132
Chapter Twenty-Four: Field On Disc 139

Afterword 143

To the memory of my parents, Nathan and Bess,
who would have loved the nocturnes had they heard them.

And to my late wife, Sandra Lee,
who gave me lessons in courage.

ACKNOWLEDGEMENTS

Every book, to a lesser or greater extent, is the product of a collaboration; and this is my moment to thank those collaborators.

The foremost exponent of John Field's music, pianist John O'Connor, graciously took time during a busy concert schedule to answer my questions. The information that Mr. O'Connor provided about the place of the nocturnes in the collective Irish psyche was especially valuable in helping to shape this book. He also referred me to important source material.

Pietro Spada, concert pianist, educator and musicologist, also took time from a busy schedule to provide information from a historical perspective that confirmed a thesis at which I had independently arrived.

Concert pianist Micheal O'Rourke, one of the current exponents of John Field's music, enlightened me with a performer's view of the nocturnes. His recorded performances often provided useful examples for analysis throughout the book.

CHAPTER ONE:

IN THE BEGINNING

Several years ago a friend presented me with a copy of Schirmer's 1902 edition of the Eighteen Nocturnes of John Field, which he had purchased for fifty cents in an antique shop. The fragile, yellowed book started a love affair with the music of a composer about whom I knew practically nothing.

After hearing on the radio several recordings of Field's Nocturnes, usually by John O'Conor, I observed that his interpretations differed markedly from the Schirmer score. Where I saw an accent, *sforzando* or crescendo, I heard none. Where the music was to be played faster, or slower, I heard no change in tempo. This disparity immediately piqued my curiosity and raised questions.

A search of the internet revealed that a Field revival had been going on for at least thirty years. Several recording companies had issued CD's of the entire works by a roster of pianists. New editions of the Nocturnes were available. And there were debates among musicologists and historians about whether or not John Field actually invented the Nocturne, and if he did, what was the source of his inspiration.

The questions continued nagging at me until I became convinced that there was enough here to warrant a full investigation of John Field and the Nocturne.

At that time, the most intriguing question focused on the Schirmer-vs.-O'Conor versions of the Nocturnes. O'Conor apparently was the premier exponent of Field's music, as well as a highly regarded musician who has recorded the thirty-two piano sonatas of Beethoven, among many other works. His expertise had to be respected. Was I misreading the scores in the Schirmer edition?

One possible explanation appeared to be the essay by Franz Liszt that introduced the first collected edition of the Nocturnes and was reprinted by

Schirmer. Liszt's conception of the music differed so utterly from mine, I concluded that generations of pianists had been influenced by that pianistic giant of the nineteenth century.

Further research modified my view. The Liszt essay was only a partial answer. I contacted John O'Conor and asked him who and what influenced his interpretations of the Nocturnes. Mr. O'Conor was gracious enough to take time from a full schedule—he was in Europe performing the entire cycle of Beethoven sonatas—to answer my questions. Following is a quote from one of his letters:

"My knowledge of Field goes back to my childhood. There is a tradition of teaching Field Nocturnes to young pianists in Ireland and the actual atmosphere is reminiscent of old Irish Airs. I met a nun once who said she had proof that many of the themes of the Nocturnes could be traced to old Irish Airs."

Clearly, the originator of the Nocturne is an Irish icon, a culture hero; and the tradition that has grown up around him is powerful. The key phrase in the above quotation is, "the actual atmosphere is reminiscent of old Irish Airs." Anyone who has heard an Irish Air knows that their principal character is a gentle lyricism, exactly the quality that John O'Conor was projecting in the Nocturnes. Consequently, Irish interpreters have established a tradition of performance that differs from Field's actual intentions (that is, from the printed score), for reasons unrelated to the Liszt essay.

Answering the question, "What is the source of the Nocturne?" is not just an academic exercise comparable to, "Who wrote the plays of Shakespeare?" The answer will affect the angle at which we view the Nocturnes, and will shape our interpretation of every phrase. If we agree with the Irish school, then these are uncomplicated bardic songs, lovely, a little sad, and consoling. If we agree with the Italian school, that the Nocturnes were inspired by the Italian song known as the "notturno," then they will be performed as melodies dressed up in fancy pianistic garments. If you agree with the Viennese school that the Nocturne comes out of the mainstream of eighteenth and early nineteenth century classical music, you will perform these lyrical pieces as though they were written by Beethoven, or Schubert, faithfully following the composer's directions.

The search for answers has been complicated by scholars and musicologists who define or describe the Nocturne quite narrowly. An example is the research of Nicholas Temperly. In his article, "John Field and the First Nocturne," published in Music and Letters, he sets as his test of the first Nocturne two characteristics: a melody with a harp-like accompaniment, the first note of which is sufficiently lower than the other notes of the broken chord that it must be caught by the pedal.

By this test, Temperly dismisses Haydn, Mozart, Clementi, Hummel and Beethoven as possible originators because the first four did not use accompaniments that exceed the span of the normal hand. Although Beethoven used broken chords in the coda of his Sonata Opus 34 (written in 1803, eleven years before Field's first Nocturnes were published) and the first note of the chord was low, in the Nocturne style, no pedal was indicated for the purpose of sustaining that note.

Based on Temperly's test, it is my sad duty to inform the reader that Field composed far fewer than the eighteen Nocturnes with which he is credited. Following the Schirmer edition's numbering: the first and second pass the test with every bar having a Nocturne bass. The third, however, does not have a single bar with the required bass and must be set aside, lovely as it is. The fourth is seventy-three bars long, but only thirty-two bars qualify. In the fifth, Field achieves a better percentage, with thirty-two of the forty-three bars qualifying. The sixth does fairly well with forty-eight out of a possible seventy-three. Unfortunately, the seventh cannot be considered a Nocturne since a paltry eight of the sixty-one bars has the prescribed bass. Number eight fares even worse, with only two out of sixty-one bars. The ninth does just as poorly, with only one out of thirty-one. From this point on, matters rapidly deteriorate, with serious consequences for John Field's reputation. The tenth, ninety bars long, has a mere two bars of the Nocturne bass; and of the remaining eight, not one has as much as a single bar.

This is a dismal record, with only two perfect Nocturnes and another three that barely gain admission into the club. If John Field was of sound mind and recognized a genuine Nocturne when he composed one, we must widen our search and even consider that the form was fashioned from several elements. Certainly the Air, with its lute-like accompaniment, is one. And the cantilena, the soothing cradlesong, may be another. Some have passages of an operatic character and are appropriately bravura and dramatic. Others sound like an adagio right out of Beethoven.

Rather early on, I was struck by the eerie presence of Beethoven. Repeated performances of the Nocturnes stimulated memories of sonatas that I had studied as a youngster. Particular passages and, in one instance, an entire Nocturne, echoed the familiar classics. By examining several sonatas of Beethoven's early and middle periods, I found the Nocturne form. It was labeled Adagio, Largo, or Andante; but if Beethoven had removed any one of them from the sonata and called it a Nocturne, he would have been credited with inventing a new form.

My central thesis, which will be developed throughout this book, is that Field is the natural son and heir of Beethoven, who gifted him with the form of the Nocturne. Field eventually wrote two kinds of Nocturne, both of which were picked up by composers throughout the Romantic period and beyond. For convenience of discussion, I call them the Introspective and the Idyllic. They are distinguished by the presence of ten characteristic figures, or motifs. The Introspective has a greater number and variety than the Idyllic. Here are the ten:

1. The yearning: a short phrase, usually three to six beats in length, in which the notes rise and retreat, often with a crescendo and *diminuendo*.
2. The sigh or sob: usually a phrase of two notes, but sometimes three or four, in which the first note is higher in pitch than the other(s), and is sometimes accented.
3. The cry or outburst: a single note, interval or chord which is struck *forte, fortissimo,* or *sforzando,* preceded and immediately followed by a subdued passage, usually *piano* or *pianissimo*.
4. The flight or release: a sudden run of 16th or 32nd notes that usually approaches or exceeds high C and may be extended for as few as three or four beats and as many as several bars.
5. Mood contrast: passages characterized by an abrupt shift from soft to loud, or the reverse; a change of mode, from major to minor, or the reverse; a marked change in tempo.
6. Mode alterations: frequent chord changes from major to minor, or the reverse, within a bar, phrase, or short passage.
7. The struggle: a sequence of syncopated or heavily accented two or three-note phrases, almost always rising.
8. The pang or stab: a chord or interval, often accented, that contains a grating or piercing element, such as a minor second. A softer effect is created by lingering chromatics whose resolution is delayed.
9. The conversation: a duet between upper and lower voices that is usually consoling.
10. The leap: a two-note phrase in which the second note is higher by at least six steps, but usually by an octave, and is often accented. This figure suggests either desperation, exuberance, or triumph, depending on the context of the passage.

I am not suggesting that any and every piece of music containing several of these motifs is a Nocturne. They must appear in a lyrical composition which is slow or leisurely in tempo, and has a particularly expressive melody, usually in single notes. The Introspective Nocturne will usually contain at least seven of the motifs, the Idyllic as few as four.

These motifs will appear throughout the book, serving as a device for revealing and releasing the authentic Nocturnes. After all the research and analysis has been completed and the questions answered, the overriding reason for writing this book is to rescue John Field and his finest creations from a troubled past. He was not an Irish waif, an innocent who wandered uninvited into the Convention Hall of Great Music. He deserves more than a footnote in musical history for popularizing the Nocturne and presenting it to Chopin to perfect. He is, rather, a gifted composer who worked within the mainstream of classical music and contributed several gems to the riches of the Romantic era.

CHAPTER TWO:

JOHN FIELD AND FRANZ LISZT

Although Franz Liszt (1811-1886) proved not to be the sole influence on the interpretation of Field's Nocturnes, he played a major role, which included relegating Field to his long-held position as a minor curiosity.

Liszt came on the scene more than a generation after John Field, who was already an acclaimed pianist when Liszt was born. The latter achieved early fame as a virtuoso and, in common with Robert Schumann, helped to promote the musical careers of promising contemporaries. He contributed significantly to the public recognition of Chopin as a composer, and also praised the originality and poetic charm of Field's Nocturnes.

It was not unexpected, then, that when the first comprehensive edition of Field's Nocturnes was assembled almost twenty years after his death, Liszt was asked to edit and write an introduction. Some reordering of the Nocturnes took place when Schirmer's edition of 1902 was printed, but the introduction was included.

I am convinced that this critical appraisal established the conventional perception of Field as a man, and shaped the interpretation of his music for generations. I cannot identify in the entire history of music another piece of writing that so profoundly affected a composer's legacy. In his essay Liszt accomplishes a remarkable feat by simultaneously extolling the virtues of his subject and relegating him to second or third-rate status and possible oblivion.

If we are to understand the fate that befell John Field and his Nocturnes, the Liszt essay requires close scrutiny. He begins with a reference to the "poignant charm of these tender poems." He speaks of their "delicate originality," "extreme simplicity of sentiment," the "charm of their spontaneity," "the simplicity of instinct which delights in the endless modulation of the simple and happy chord of the sentiment with which the heart is filled." His Nocturnes are "an incomparable model of grace unconscious of itself, of melancholy artlessness." ". . . a perfection of incomparable naivete . . . shy and serenely tender emotions . . ." Liszt almost surpasses himself when he compares the Nocturnes to ". . . those pearly shells that open, far from the tempests and immensities of Ocean, beside some murmuring spring shaded by the palms of a happy oasis which makes us forget even the existence of the desert."

Liszt seems to have an inexhaustible supply of poetic phrases with which to depict music that is almost ethereal and otherworldly, that has only a tenuous connection with the experiences and emotions of the rest of humanity. In the latter part of the essay, when he is approaching his summation, he recalls his childhood impressions of the Nocturnes. He spent hours indulging in ". . . the soothing influences of the visions flowing from the gentle intoxication of this music . . . hallucinations free from fever and violent emotion, but filled, on the contrary, with floating iridescent images whose touching beauties, in some moments of happy illusion, reach the intensity of passion."

Liszt neglects to mention that, in addition to passages of delicacy and beauty, these lyrical pieces also contain the powerful emotions of a real person, anguish, darkness and inconsolable melancholy. But Liszt goes even further. In describing the music, he begins to assemble a portrait of the composer as naïve, artless, unconscious of self, shy, instinctive, as precious as his music.

Liszt continues this bloodless assassination by painting a portrait of Field, the man. Here are some representative statements: "Both in writing and in playing, his sole idea was fully to express his own conceptions to himself; one cannot imagine a franker disregard if the public than was his." "It was easy to see that his chief auditor was himself. His tranquility was well nigh somnolent." The portrait comes into sharper focus with this judgment: "Field sang to and for himself, and his own enjoyment sufficed him; he asked nothing more of music. He wrote, as it were, for pastime . . . One is led to the belief that . . . he but sought to satisfy his own imaginative faculty—creating without effort, perfecting without trouble, and publishing with indifference."

An indifferent, somnolent hobbyist? Liszt knew better. As an observer of Field's life and editor of his work, Liszt had to have known that several versions of the Nocturnes existed, some with dozens of bars excised, or added. Field was a compulsive critic of his own work. This fact alone puts the lie to Liszt's characterization.

Having thus exposed his hapless and helpless subject, Liszt closes his essay with enough damning praise to put a padlock on the door of the basement room to which he has consigned John Field. "Are not his nocturnes half-waking dreams, in a night without gloom?" "Field's entire life (was) exempt . . . from the burning rays projected by vivid passions, and flowing on in dreamy idleness . . . like a long nocturne without the lightening of any storm, and wherein no blustering tempest ever marred the calm of reposeful nature."

Depicted as a sort of humanoid dropped off by visiting aliens, Field is all but stripped of his personhood and humanity. All this despite Liszt's sharing in the common knowledge that Field suffered the trauma of a bad marriage that finally ended when is wife left him, taking their son to a distant city; that he was so frequently inebriated that he became known as "Drunken John"; and that he went into a creative decline for about ten years, during which he composed almost nothing and gradually drank himself into a terminal illness.

Near the close of the essay, Liszt administers the coup de grace in a lengthy passage that compares Field and Chopin. Although a number of Field's successors ". . . brought the Nocturne to greater heights," Chopin was the one genius who ". . . in his poetic nocturnes, sang not only the harmonies which are the source of our most ineffable delights, but likewise the restless, agitating bewilderment to which they oft give rise. His flight is loftier, though his wing be more wounded; and his very suaveness grows heartrending, so thinly does it veil his despairful anguish . . . Their closer kinship to sorrow than those of Field renders them the more strongly marked; their poetry is more somber and fascinating; they ravish us more, but are less reposeful . . ."

The astonishing irony is that the virtues attributed to Chopin are equally true of Field.

The final paragraph of this notorious essay contains a summation that Liszt might have had inscribed as Field's epitaph, had he been called upon to do so:

"He will ever be an incomparable model of grace unconscious of itself, of melancholy artlessness."

For approximately a century and a quarter, Liszt succeeded in diminishing the reputation of Field almost to the point of oblivion. Interest in Field's music was confined almost exclusively to the Nocturnes; and by the last decade of the nineteenth century, they, too, were largely forgotten. When Schirmer decided to reissue the Nocturnes, they may have looked upon Field as an interesting curiosity, a composer of some historical importance worth adding to their catalogue.

This Liszt affair does raise a fascinating question. What was his motivation? Ignorance of the music is impossible to consider. Field not only compulsively revised his music, he provided precise and copious notations in order to avoid any misjudgment of his intent. As editor of the edition, Liszt was given the charge of closely examining every bar, every phrase, every note. Even a pianist of far less astuteness and sensitivity—say, a reasonably talented intermediate student—would discover a more authentic John Field in those pages than the one depicted in the essay.

The answer may be found in that long paragraph in which Liszt compares Field to Chopin, to the distinct advantage of the latter. His motive certainly could not have been an attempt to boost the career of Chopin, who was several years deceased when the essay was written, and whose reputation had been solidly established. It is difficult to be charitable at this point. If Liszt knew that his depiction of the Nocturnes was false, and if he benefited neither himself nor anyone else by this deception, his only motive had to be an attempt to diminish the achievement of Field. For what purpose?

This brings us back to Chopin, whose stature was enhanced, in part, by the fiction that he developed and perfected a form that was in its infancy. Liszt hammers home this view in the final lines of his essay: "He is one of those types of a primitive, with which one meets only at certain artistic epochs, when art, beginning to devine her resources has not yet exhausted them . . ."

The truth, which Liszt so skillfully concealed, is that Chopin borrowed all the essentials from Field, both style and emotional expressiveness, which were inseparable. (An exhaustive study of this debt has been done by David Branson in his book, *John Field and Frederick Chopin*.) Having publicly invested himself in Chopin, Liszt quite naturally had an interest in preserving his own reputation. But he may have had an additional motive, that of simple revenge. It was well known, certainly in musical circles, that Field was openly contemptuous of Chopin's music, and possibly of his performance as a pianist. He described Chopin as "un talent de chamber de malade," a sickroom talent. As a performer, Chopin so hated to play loud enough to be heard in the rear of the hall, he gave up concertizing early in his career. And many of his short pieces, such as the nocturnes and preludes, are quite lyrical and delicate. But these, of course, are balanced by the numerous pieces that are brilliant, energetic and dynamic.

Another motive may be more personal. Field was known to be brilliant and inventive in repartee. He was also an inveterate punster. In his excellent book, *"The Life and Music of John Field,"* Patrick Piggott relates that when Field attended his first Franz Liszt concert, he turned to his companion and asked loudly, "Does he bite?" This was in response to the fierce bravura manner in which Liszt attacked the keyboard. The mot made the rounds of the salons and coffee houses, and no doubt found its way, eventually, to Liszt.

His essay, which Liszt suspected—or at least hoped—would dog Field for years, may have been payback.

CHAPTER THREE:

JOHN FIELD, F.J. HAYDN, AND W.A. MOZART

Haydn, along with Mozart and Beethoven, was one of the most celebrated and successful composers of his era. He was adored in London, where he composed his last symphonies. He was also one of the composers whom Field openly declared he made a point of not introducing to his students. Was this strange exclusion a tacit inference that the music of Haydn was inferior and unworthy of study? There is no record that Field offered any explanation.

If I were to suggest that his unstated motivation was to conceal his debt to Haydn, similar to his debt to Beethoven, the reader would be justifiably skeptical, if not baffled. What could Haydn, the composer of such sprightly, symmetrical, good-natured and sometimes humorous music, contribute to the making of the nocturne? I am unaware of any publication that draws a connection between Haydn and Field. One likely reason is that Haydn never wrote any piano music with the "nocturne bass," mentioned in Chapter One. The other, even more persuasive factor, is that in temperament and musical language, the two men were just too different.

It has been said that Beethoven's piano sonatas were the laboratory in which he worked out ideas which he developed more fully in his orchestral and chamber works. The possibility that Haydn did the same led me to reexamine the last twenty-five of his fifty-two sonatas. This task was strongly motivated by the hunch that in those later sonatas, mostly composed after 1780, I would uncover what Field was determined to conceal.

There was, indeed, a great deal to conceal. The Adagio of Haydn's Sonata No. 46 alone was enough to keep Field awake nights praying that none of his students, out of perverse curiosity, would go out and purchase a copy. If performed at an appropriately slow tempo, and if the upper voice is sung soulfully, this could be taken for one of Beethoven's Adagios from the middle period. The variety of textures, the plaintive melody, the delicate yet expressive use of the inner voices, the daring and inspired harmonic sequences, the urgency of chromatics and passing tones, the wistful yearning—it is all pure romanticism, without reservation or qualification.

Oh, to have seen Field's expression when he first played this Adagio, particularly the sixteen-bar passage beginning at bar 29. Despite the presence of two lower voices, the melody sounds melancholy and alone. It occasionally rises a third, but its identifying character is a descending scale, a mixture of diatonic and chromatic longing. This downward movement is accompanied by a constantly shifting harmonic sequence, chords usually altered by chromatic passing tones. The key is D-flat, but this section begins in the dominant, which becomes B-flat, G7, E-flat7, A-flat, D dim., E-flat minor, A-flat dim., and F7. The subtle nuances are so unclassical, they may have struck Field with an awe of biblical proportions.

Midway through this sixteen-bar passage, the lone upper voice begins to climb, slowly, tentatively, in 8th notes. When it arrives at high C, the scale—now only three successive notes—rises instead of descends. The two lower voices move into the treble clef to support the singer. But even at that height there is unmistakable longing and pathos in the song. After four bars, the three voices slowly descend, through major and minor harmonies, back to the tonic D-flat.

Field needed to hear only those sixteen bars to unlock the emotions that clamored for a voice. In that passage, aside from whatever else he wrote, Haydn laid bare the soul of Romantic expression and the Introspective Nocturne.

The closing nine bars of this Adagio probably caught Field's attention as well. Essentially it is a cadence that suspends its resolution for six bars. It begins on D-flat minor with a thematic figure consisting mostly of repeated 8th notes interrupted in each bar by one beat given to a figure in 32nd or 16th notes. Despite the breaks, it is rather static. From D-flat minor the harmony passes through E, A-flat, A, G-flat minor, E-flat, and finally to the tonic. The harmony gives this passage its drama and suspense, right up to the crescendo that ends *forte* on the dominant.

The slow movements of these later sonatas are truly exploratory. In each, Haydn took a different path. The Adagio of No. 39 emphasizes the melodic line and the constant drift of harmony and passing tones. But, in common with all of the slow movements, no figure or design prevails for more than eight bars. Always there is an impulse toward contrast and variety. In this

Adagio, after four bars of soulful singing, the melody will take off on a flight of grace notes, or 16th notes aloft, either singly or in thirds. The rich harmony of three or four inner voices will be replaced by a single voice in the bass. In short, the classic ideal of symmetry, cohesion and restraint is abandoned for the impulsive, the personal, the adventurous.

The Andante of Sonata No. 42 is the opening movement. This in itself was a significant break with the classic form, a step that Mozart also took about three years later. Marked *con espressione,* this movement must be performed at around MM quarter note=63, which is actually in the adagio range. This Andante appears to be driven by a desire to push dynamics to their outer limits. Starting *piano,* in the third bar we have three explosive *sforzandos*—before we have gotten comfortably settled in our seats. Throughout the opening section and the development that follows, *fortes* and *sforzandos* are abruptly followed by delicate and graceful phrases, *piano.* Three chords are marked *fortissimo sforzando,* about the loudest sound one can produce on the piano with those particular notes. By examining the score, the reader will find other types of contrast that Haydn employed in what appears to be his attempt to stretch, and possibly snap, the bonds of classicism.

What has all this to do with the Nocturne? The answer, at least in part, is that Haydn provided Field with a new language for expressing powerful emotion and the freedom, the permission, to take his own path, wherever it might lead.

Before moving on to Mozart, let us take a look at the Adagio movement of Sonata No. 52. It resembles the No. 42 Andante in that it begins *piano* and by the third bar it rises to *forte.* In both, the thematic line also rises immediately. Again the dynamic range is pushed, but No. 52 prefers *fortissimos* to *sforzandos.*

After the first sixteen bars, the difference begins to assert itself. In this Adagio, the dynamic extremes are not as important as the range and swiftness of movement. In bar 20, the upper and lower voices are in the bass clef, performing an energetic duet, an octave apart. This quickly ends with a stream of grace notes that begin at E below middle C and climb, within the span of one beat, to E above high C, a flight of three octaves. Some graceful acrobatics in 32nd notes occupy the next two bars, followed by a chromatic run of grace notes in the treble, a duet of grace notes an octave lower, and then chromatic grace notes solo in the bass, the latter spanning an octave in half a beat.

In similar fashion, the notes fly between the lowest range of the keyboard in Haydn's time to above high C. The swooping phrases that act as connecting links between the other musical figures are always played *forte* This sort of youthful exuberance and elation seems to be a celebration of freedom from the last bonds of classical restraint and moderation.

After Field witnessed all this, was it possible for him to believe that there was anything he could not do?

When Mozart died on March 4, 1791, John Field was four-and-a-half months shy of his ninth birthday. By age eleven he was apprenticed to Muzio Clemente, who undertook his education, both as pianist and composer. There can be no doubt that among Field's music lessons during the next several years was the study of at least several of Mozart's nineteen sonatas for piano.

In the slow movements of every piano sonata Mozart wrote are the building blocks that Field used, some variant of those motifs described in Chapter One. Mozart's use of the slow movement is a fascinating phenomenon. Here was the theater in which he could be expansive and—within the bounds of current taste—more self-indulgent and emotive. He seized his opportunities, even within the theme-and-variation form.

The third movement of Sonata No. 9 is an excellent example. Marked Andante, all of the twelve variations except Numbers XI and XII are seventeen bars long, eight in the principal section, nine in the development. The last variation is an exuberant finale that fittingly breaks the mold, complete with *fortissimos* and several *sforzandos* (the latter appearing in only two other variations). The Adagio variation has nothing in common with all the others, neither in form, length, thematic development, or emotive content. It might have been written for another sonata and inserted here. Instead, we find motif #1 seven times; motif #2 eight times; motif #3 eight times; motif #4 five times; motif #6 nine times; motif #7 twice; motif #8 eight times; and motif #10 six times.

An equally rich source of introspective constructions can be found in the Adagio of the unnumbered late Sonata in C minor, K 457. Emotively and structurally this is the most complex movement of all the nineteen sonatas. The frequent and dramatic alterations of mood suggest an ambivalence and conflict that is rare in the piano literature of the classical period. If the reader doubts that Mozart had, toward the end, walked into the realm of romanticism not tentatively but with sturdy self assurance, please listen attentively to this Adagio, as well as Sonata No. 14, K300d, and the Fantasia, K 475.

All of this intense expressiveness could not have escaped the attention of the youthful John Field, who was looking beyond the strict classical training of Clementi for his own identity and voice.

The Adagio of the Sonata in C minor begins in E-flat with the peaceful moonlit stroll that characterizes the opening section of several Field Nocturnes before he unleashes his darker, moody side. The Adagio begins not *piano* but *sotto voce*. By bar 2 we know that this story is going to take an unexpected turn. Without foreshadowing, Mozart is singing his theme *forte*, motif #5. These are also long, yearning phrases, motif #1, spanning two bars. In contrast to the *forte*, there are, alternately, dainty 16th or 32nd notes played *portamento*. This interplay between the two voices, one delicate, the other assertive, continues through the first 22 bars. If performed exactly as Mozart directed, this has to be unsettling. This music is so densely emotive, one could stop at almost every bar to examine the process.

In bars 5 and 6 there is a sequence of three sighs in an unusual variant, a phrase of five 32nd notes descending *portamento*. These stand in contrast to the rising 32nd notes that preceded. In bar 11 the first flight, motif #4, begins *piano* and ends, after a brief struggle, at F above high C, *forte* and accented. This volatility intensifies with shifting harmonies contributing to the drama, motif #6. Notes rise in G minor, climax in B-flat, then descend in D dim. on the second beat, change to C minor on the third beat, and E minor with a lowered fifth and minor seventh, then back to B-flat.

In bars 12-13, the conversation, motif #9, appears as 32nd note phrases that alternate between bass and treble voices in three sets. At the third repetition we have our first motif #3, a *forte* that follows a *piano* without a crescendo. This outburst is immediately followed by three groups of four 32nd notes, alternating sighs with their struggle upward to F above high C, motif #7. At the apex there begins a sequence of three sighs, in both treble and bass, *mancando*, dying away. Mozart could have posted a *diminuendo* but his choice emphasizes the dramatic and poignant nature of this passage.

Then, immediately after a *pianissimo*, Mozart surprises in the way that Field often does in his Nocturnes: *sforzandos* alternately in bass and treble, then *piano,* and we are back to the opening theme, gentle and lilting, as though nothing had happened.

But something remarkable is going on, a kind of confessional. "In vino veritas" can be restated as "in adagio veritas." In the great music of the past, before music tended to become, in the twentieth century, largely impersonal, the man inhabited his creation. John Field needed such habitation, and he was finding the means through his study of the classical masters in their most intimate moments.

The surprises in this Adagio don't stop coming. When the main theme reappears, the bass notes are now octaves, rising in a crescendo against treble notes that are just a half beat behind, emphasizing effort, struggle, and determination, motif #7. More *forte-piano* contrasts follow. A new subject is introduced, in which the melody hovers around middle C, and the bass figure descends to its lowest point, A-flat two octaves below middle C. The melody gradually rises in a series of crescendos and *diminuendos* until an outburst on the dominant B-flat chord, a high A-flat heavily accented, and then an extraordinary display of 32nd and 64th grace notes swooping down two octaves, then up almost three full octaves, and finally down after cresting *forte* with a sharply accented E-flat.

This tonal artifact encompasses the full range of a man's emotions, aspirations and vision, from the abyss to the heights. One may argue that Mozart was only striving for an effect, and any attempt to divine the personal in an artifice is misguided. Since this is not a science, one can only look at the evidence and come to a reasonable conclusion. The author firmly believes, after much careful examination of many scores, that a new musical vocabulary was being formed during the classical period, and that it flowered in the romantic period, evolving through Mozart, Haydn, Beethoven, Schubert and Field to Chopin, Schumann and others.

Try to imagine the effect that music such as this must have had on Field, and the vistas of musical expression that were revealed to him. Any reader who accepts my thesis as valid can never again look at John Field in the same way, or accept the anemic fairyland interpretation of his Nocturnes advocated by Liszt.

We have traveled a great distance from the song-like opening theme of this slow movement. Perhaps to emphasize his point, Mozart follows the last descending line of grace notes with four-note descending phrases which are another variant of motif #2; but these are sobs of a quite wrenching kind. The uncommon dynamic fp occurs on the second of four 16th notes, which requires that the second 16th be struck *forte* and the third and fourth *piano*. Thus we have a syncopated figure of dramatic contrasts, supported by accented sighs in the bass. Again, the thematic number is three repetitions.

The next noteworthy feature immediately follows. This is the six-bar passage that employs chromatics in the middle and lower voices, while the melody moves above, usually separated by five or six steps from the lower voices. In the first two bars of this passage the chromatics are not stressed, but in bars 3-6 they carry accents, which makes them dynamically equivalent to the melody, an example of motif #9. At the same time, the melody is forming motifs #1, 2 and 7 in quick succession, repeated the three magical times. With so much going on, this is almost orchestral in its complexity. Similar passages can be found in Field's Nocturnes, numbers 3, 10, 13, 14, 15 and 16.

In each of the six bar phrases cited above, we also find a constant dramatic crescendo to *forte,* and down to *piano.* At the end, after struggling upward, motif #7, there is an octave leap to high C, motif #10, and a brief progression up to E-flat above high C. This is not desperation but rather a moment of triumphant accomplishment. What follows is also extraordinary. It seems that a sort of membrane has been broken, a written-out arpeggio, one might say, uniformly *piano* until the second half of the second bar. Here a crescendo begins, peaks *forte* on high B-flat, and descends gradually to B-flat below middle C. The descent is mostly in the B-flat scale, with several chromatics interspersed, in keeping with the character of this section.

The principal theme returns at bar 41. There is a brief duet, a repetition of the alternating sighs, upward and downward flights of 32nd notes, another octave leap to high C, bar 50, another dramatic descent from B-flat below high C to B-flat two octaves below middle C. In bar 52, when we reach the nadir, a brilliant shower of 64th notes rises *presto* to F above high C.

The final five bars lull us into believing that the emotionally draining journey is over, and we can peacefully sink into our easy chair. But Mozart is concerned only with his own sensibilities. *Piano* is followed by *forte, pianissimo* is followed by another *forte.* Finally, with two sighs, *smorzando* and then *pianissimo,* it is over.

Field learned a certain gracefulness and fluidity of expression from Mozart. But he also discovered that some of his more personal—and carefully concealed—emotions could find expression in musical form. This learning process continued to expand and deepen as he matured, but it began very early with his exposure to Mozart. In the slow movements of Mozart's piano sonatas, he surely found demonstrated that deep emotion can be expressed with relatively simple means.

For much too long, Mozart suffered from the same preconceptions that continue to afflict Field. As a classicist, it was generally assumed that Mozart separated the private self from the brilliant outpouring of perfectly crafted pieces in almost every known form. Not until the twentieth century did a new school of thought insist that the reversals of fortune in Mozart's life, his financial problems, the periods of separation and loneliness, the loss of loved ones, found expression in his music.

CHAPTER FOUR:

JOHN FIELD AND L. van BEETHOVEN

In his biography of Field, Patrick Piggott relates that Field emphatically declared his indifference to the piano music of Beethoven. He is quoted as describing it as "a German dish rag." Translation: dull, drab, and uninspired.

While under the tutelage of Clementi during the 1790's, Field was exposed to a rigid classical training that included Bach (he is reputed to have memorized and performed from memory the entire Well Tempered Clavier), Haydn, Mozart and Beethoven. Clementi's publisher in Paris kept him supplied with the latest publications of classical music. When Clementi arranged for the publication of Field's first three sonatas in 1802, his student accompanied him to Paris. By 1802, the first sixteen of Beethoven's piano sonatas had been published. Field's knowledge of them during his London years and later, in Paris, can scarcely be doubted.

Despite Field's professed indifference to the sonatas of Beethoven, his influence can be detected in several of his compositions. Listen to Field's first sonata. The principal theme of the first movement begins in the genial mood of Mozart. About midway, during the development section, Beethoven barges in. The melodic line, which had been floating lightheartedly above, is suddenly grounded and meshes with the darker, louder chords in the lower register. Then, abruptly as he arrived, Ludwig departs without a farewell.

If there had been a fourth sonata in 1802, Clementi undoubtedly would have arranged to publish it with the other three. When it did appear, the first of the two movements is marked Moderato. As performed, with compelling sensitivity, by John O'Conor, the opening section is actually adagio, MM quarter note=63. This music, which takes the listener on an emotional journey of contrasting light and dark, heights and depths, calm and agitation, is the work of a mature and accomplished composer who has found his voice.

It is, in fact, Field's first Nocturne. And it is also the natural child of Beethoven, whose adagios are present in almost every bar. When Field heard those soulful slow movements, particularly in the sonatas of Beethoven's middle period, his exposure to the language of profound personal expression was complete. What he found in its more temperate form in the Mozart sonatas emerged more powerfully and in much darker hues in those of Beethoven.

The ensuing chapters of this book, which deal with the individual Nocturnes, will trace the influence of Beethoven from his Opus 2 onward, and especially his Opus 10 No. 3, Opus 13, Opus 22, and Opus 27 No. 2.

We turn our attention to the Adagio of Opus 22, which contains all ten of the motifs. Does this mean that Beethoven invented the nocturne years before the form was christened by Field? The evidence that he did is compelling. This Adagio is as close to the romantic nocturne as one can find, prior to Field and Chopin. That Beethoven did not call it a nocturne, or set it forth as a separate piece, is far less important than his having created a short, lyrical form of intimate personal expression.

The Opus 22 Adagio begins with the yearning phrase, motif #1, which occurs in bars 1-2, 2-3, 3-4 and 4-5. The first six beats of the fourth occurrence are combined with motif #4, a flight that is tentative and never goes very far. At the end of bar 5, motif #4 returns briefly, attaining the B-flat below high C. As it returns, the emotional level rises with a crescendo and a leap of two octaves to high C, *sforzando*, motif #10. This is an example of an extended and quite dramatic motif #1, a characteristic grand gesture of Beethoven's that is also found in Field. An example is in the final sixteen bars of Nocturne No. 2 in E-flat.

The sigh, motif #2, follows almost immediately in bar 8, first in a two-note phrase, then in six three-note phrases. Without pause, we move on to motif #3, a succession of three *sforzando* chords followed by a *pianissimo* sigh. In bar 13 we have another yearning phrase that concludes with a sigh, a combination of motifs #1 and 2. In the same bar a lower voice enters, supporting the upper and forming a brief duet, motif #9. Also in bar 13, a yearning phrase returns, peaks with a *sforzando* that also forms the first note of a sob, followed by an uninterrupted succession of five more sobs.

The first example of motif #7, the struggle, appears in bars 22-23, six two-note phrases moving upward chromatically. This is an expression of yearning that is forlorn and apparently doomed. But it is followed, in bars 24-

26, by release and flight, motif #4, which crescendos to the F above high C, *sforzando*. Thus, the drama of the Introspective Nocturne begins to unfold.

In bar 27 we find motifs #1 and 3 combined in a yearning phrase that rises to a *sforzando,* an expression of pain and desperation that is repeated in bar 28. A three-note variation of motif #2 follows and is repeated four times. The last repetition ends *poco ritardando*, suggesting a moment of resignation.

Bar 31 is an example of motif #5, an abrupt change of key without any modulation. We go from a B-flat chord in bar 30 to a G in 31. But what appears to be a relief from the emotional stress of the first thirty bars is short lived. One of the revolutionary changes in harmony that Beethoven introduced occurs in bar 32. It is an F dim.9 arrived at chromatically with the fifth of the chord a half step lower and accented, resolving three beats later. The 9th is also emphasized by the repeated octaves on G in the bass. This is an excellent example of motif #8, the thrust or pang, somewhat muted by the *pianissimo*. The same motif occurs in bar 33, where an E7 clashes with the repeated G in the bass. At beat number four it is resolved into a G7.

Immediately we enter a six-bar passage that combines motifs #1 and 3. The upper voice rises and falls, but octaves in the bass counter with *sforzando* thrusts on the first beat of each bar. Beethoven never allows more than a bar or two of relief. The drama continues to unfold, shifting or lunging from one motif to another in a masterful piece of writing that wrings all the emotion possible from the material, yet achieves a level of sublimity.

Beethoven's exposition of the nocturne is more robust, assertive and darker than Field's. The latter was foremost a melodist and a singer; thus the texture of his music is more lyrical and usually (with some notable exceptions) less dramatic than Beethoven's. But the differences are ones of personality. Beethoven's innovations in highly emotive music, which came to be known as romanticism, were filtered through Field's psyche.

Field's Nocturne Number Nine is a bold appropriation of Beethoven's Opus 27 No. 2 Adagio. But this is atypical of how Field absorbed, assimilated and re-structured what he acquired from Beethoven, as well as other sources. The process can be illustrated by juxtaposing Field's fourth Nocturne and the Adagio of Beethoven's Opus 22.

It is interesting to note that the fourth and ninth are the only Nocturnes marked Adagio. Since the fourth does not share the same key or meter with the Opus 22, one may be inclined to dismiss any significant connection between them. As we might expect, they both have the graceful, dignified, soulful melody found in most adagios. But there are other, non-typical characteristics that these two pieces have in common.

Beethoven, in bar 22, suddenly interrupts the melodic flow with a sequence of six two-note phrases, each with stresses on the first note, that rise and fall. In bar 11, Field has four two-note phrases with accents on the first note, ascending. Beethoven, in bars 25-26, suddenly interrupts the melodic flow with an extended run of 32nd notes. Field, in bar 20, interrupts the melody with eight triplets in 32nd notes, followed by eight 64th notes. In bar 31, after a *ritardando* and four beats of silence, Beethoven—without modulation—goes into a new key, although there is no change of key signature. After a transitional passage of three bars marked *piangendo* (crying), Field goes from A to C minor, without modulating. After a seven-bar transition, Beethoven develops his theme within a strikingly different setting. It is heard in single notes in the upper voice, accompanied by two lower voices in 16th notes moving restlessly in close formation, each beat progressing up or down the scale by whole or half steps. In bar 30, Field has the theme on top and 16th notes progressing in units of six (two triplets) up and down the scale.

In both compositions there is a sequence of crescendos and *diminuendos*, a constant swelling and subsiding. But Field injects considerably more passion into his development section. He tosses the theme from treble to bass and back, with a powerful *forte* passage buttressed by chords in the bass just before a *diminuendo* that leads to a *sforzando* at bar 40 and eight more bars of roiling 16ths. In this passage, Field uses two more elements of the Beethoven Adagio. The repeated E-flat in bars 60-61 (treble) and bars 65-68 (bass) appear as F-sharp in bars 44-46 of the Nocturne. The two-note phrases with stress on the first note occur in the Opus 22 in bars 16, 17, 61-64, 69 and 70. Also with accents or stress on the first note, they occur in bars 11, 46-49, and 62 in the Nocturne.

Beside these thematic and structural similarities, both compositions are alike in mood and atmosphere. In this instance, Field goes beyond Beethoven in passion. The middle section of the fourth Nocturne is the longest and emotionally the most intense of all eighteen. It is as though Field had tapped some reservoir at the deepest level of his psyche.

Beethoven's Sonata Opus 2 No. 1, published in 1795 and written during his early twenties, already speaks in the language and voice of romanticism. One has only to turn to the Adagio, marked *cantabile* and *dolce*, to find the distinctive musical elements that will later inhabit the work of Field, Chopin, and numerous contemporaries. The song of the poet above, the moving repetitive accompaniment below, the constant rise and fall of the phrases, the extended flight of 16th and 32nd notes, the duet, the sighs and the struggle—at least one of the ten motifs will be found in every bar.

In his introductory essay, Liszt offered one significant insight. This was his observation that ". . . the Nocturne . . . bears our thoughts at the outset toward those hours wherein the soul, released from all the cares of the day, is lost in self-contemplation . . ."

More accurately, the soul is released from the demands and distractions of the day, and in the quiet solitude of night can contemplate his life, his world, his emotions, his hope and his pain. His response to this experience of self-contemplation is the musical poem that Field chose to call Nocturne. Most often it is filled with the cares of the day and the emotions they arouse, unlike the extraordinary flight of fancy with which Liszt completes and illustrates his observation. The soul, he says, ". . . soars toward the regions of a starlit heaven. We see her hovering on ethereal pinions, like the antique Philomela, over the flowers and perfumes of a nature whereof she is enamoured." And so on.

Liszt's description may be true, in part, of the Idyllic Nocturne. But the Introspective is grounded and speaks about the ache and aspiration of being human on the level plane of reality in a very real world.

The Largo Appassionato of Beethoven's Sonata Opus 2 No. 2 has several of the nocturnal motifs, but it is not of a character that would appeal to Field or be of much service to him. This Largo is almost funereal in its heavy-footed, brooding and alternately defiant and despairing outbursts. The flight that brings release, even temporarily, is not here; and this soaring of the poet's voice was essential to Field's Irish nature.

The Adagio of Opus 2, No. 3 is also full of dark and somber hues, but almost from the start, after the eight-bar statement of the yearning theme in E major, the phrases aspire upward, and to the accompaniment of a repetitive line of 32nd notes in E minor, a fragment of melody vaults from the bass to D above high C. All the drama that one comes to expect from the Introspective Nocturne is here; and it only grows more intense, from *fortissimo* to *piano* and back, with minor seconds *forte* and accented, as voices in the upper and lower regions insistently and passionately question and answer each other. A return to the contemplative theme in E-major promises some relief, resolution, perhaps even comfort. But the demons have not left, and we go through the experience once again, just as fiercely, with a constant rising and falling of voices.

Toward the close, we hear the fateful pulsation of a B repeated nineteen times in unaltered rhythm. With the *pianissimo* sigh at the end, nothing is resolved. We are given just a glimpse, a few minutes in duration, into the soul of the poet. That it resonates in some magical and indefinable way in our own psyche is one of the mysteries of music. That it resonated for John Field can hardly be doubted. In this Adagio he found all ten of the motifs that speak to us so eloquently in his Introspective Nocturnes.

Turning to his Nocturne No. 1, we find repeated notes in a passage of yearning and struggle, where they serve as a somber counterpoint. Repeated notes also appear in Nocturne No. 5, occur twelve separate times, and form a secondary motif as the upper voice rises and descends in a long line. This repetitive figure shows up in Nocturne No. 6 and, of course, in No. 9, the near-parody of Beethoven's Opus 27 No. 2, where repeated notes form the secondary theme.

In Nocturne No. 11, this repetitive figure intensifies the drama toward the close, where a B-flat below middle C is repeated fifteen times during an intensely emotive passage that combines struggle and sobbing. Very much in the spirit of this Adagio of Beethoven's, a high G figures prominently in Nocturne No. 13. In the last twenty-two bars this note is struck on each beat in three bars, and on the first beat in seven bars. This same G is struck on the first beat of forty-four other bars, for a grand total of fifty-four bars in a Nocturne ninety-eight bars long.

Nocturne No. 16 is the best example of the use of repeated notes to create a counter voice as the melody rises and falls, yearns and struggles. Passages in this Nocturne could have been written by Beethoven.

The Adagio of the Opus 10 No. 1 also contains all ten motifs of the Introspective Nocturne, in multiple repetitions. Only motif #6, alteration of mode, plays an insignificant role here. This moody and agitated Adagio is remarkable in that Beethoven achieves almost all of his effects while remaining with the key of A-flat. His inventive use of the other nine motifs creates his drama.

The sequence of triplets in which the second note rises and the third falls, or just the reverse, is an important motif in this Adagio, and it appears in several of Field's Nocturnes. A miniature version of motif #1, it is everywhere in Nocturne No. 1, in both treble and bass. In Nocturne No. 2, this triplet runs throughout the bass line, and occurs quite dramatically in the treble near the end, where the first note of the triplet is a 16th rest, and the second note is accented. In Nocturne No. 3, the triplet occurs frequently, but almost always dropping on the second note. This motif plays a major role in Nocturne No. 11, which is in 12/8 meter. If written in ¾, we would have a relentless succession of triplets rising on the second note. There are contrasting passages in which the triplet rises in the form of a triad, thus supporting the changes in mood that characterize almost all of the Nocturnes.

Equipped with the ten motifs, the reader will find parallels throughout the slow movements of Beethoven's piano sonatas. They are the basic vocabulary of lyrical, introspective expression.

CHAPTER FIVE:

NOCTURNE NO. 1

Before we begin a detailed analysis of the first Nocturne, I must encourage the reader to obtain a copy of the Schirmer edition of the Eighteen Nocturnes. Other editions, such as Peters and Kalmus, are readily available; but the Schirmer, despite its flaws, is the most reliable and the closest to Field's conception of these pieces. A copy can be obtained from Breitkoph and Hartel, through the internet.

As a means of entrance into the world of these Nocturnes, I have invented a drama. No inference is being made that John Field was conscious of this or any other drama during the creative process. In common with most artists who work with an abstract medium, he composed in collaboration with a non-verbal, emotional source of inspiration. The drama, or story, that I invent for each Nocturne is merely a useful device; and the reader may, eventually, invent his or her own versions.

Each drama plays out on three levels, starting from the bass clef and working up to the highest register. The bass, up to middle C, is the self and the reality in which the self exists. It is the world that we are compelled to inhabit and to which we must always return. For the John Field of these Nocturnes, this world is a foreign country in which he feels emotionally alienated and often desperately sad. The second level is the voice of the private John Field, to whom I refer as "the poet" or "the singer." This voice is Field's only vehicle of expression, his means of coping with loneliness and despair. He sings because through song he is momentarily released of his earthly bonds and free to be his authentic self. The third level is the register stretching approximately from the second G above middle C upward. This is the zone of aspiration, of release, of visions, of unfettered joy, each identifiable by the context of the story.

There are no sharp demarcations of these levels, and Field the poet/singer moves fluidly, often rapidly, from one to another, his voice rising and falling above the constantly moving voices below. The implication for the pianist is clear. He must first be a singer, because the song is the soul of John Field the poet, spinning in sound a coded message of his emotions.

The poet also has an alter ego with whom he sometimes carries on a dialogue. They are both involved in the poet's desire to rise above his earthly condition as often and for as long as possible. His state of mind, his attempts to take flight, and the nature of the flight are the essential elements of the drama.

This outline is not a depiction or summation of Field's actual life, which was in various ways much more complex. This device is an attempt to evoke only what Field expressed in the language of music. I will examine each Nocturne, identify the ten motifs as they appear, and show how they convey the unfolding story. No two are alike, and each requires an individual interpretive approach and performance strategy.

Dr. Baker's introductory essay, found in the 1902 Schirmer edition, concludes by describing Field's Nocturnes as portraying ". . . subjective and profound emotion . . . and from them the inspired interpreter and rapt listener will be able to learn far more of Field's true soul-life than can be taught by a few lines of plain prose."

That is worth reading several times, because it is probably the most perceptive statement ever written about John Field and his music. But it would be hotly disputed by Liszt and the entire Irish school. Of the first Nocturne, Liszt says: "The first and fifth Nocturnes in this collection are marked by a radiant happiness, one might say an overflowing felicity, evoked without exertion, and enjoyed with pure delight."

After first reading that statement, my thoughts ran along the following lines: Mind boggling! To which piece of music was Liszt actually referring? The *first* Nocturne? Really? Was this after a heavy meal, including too much wine?

In his biography of John Field, Patrick Piggott includes these descriptive phrases in his analysis of the first Nocturne: ". . . a type of melodic line which suggests the bel canto of an Italian singer . . ." ". . . preference for decoration rather than development, the lack of contrast and modulation . . ." ". . . a short codetta . . . very suggestive of the instrumental ritornellos of a vocal romance . . ." "The decorations . . . are exactly what the music needs to intensify its poetic effect without altering its mood." "Though nothing could be less complicated than this nocturne, it bears, for all its apparent naivety, the hallmark of a perfect work of art . . ."

For quite some time I was astonished by these misreadings of Nocturne Number One. But after studying all eighteen, it became clear to me that by comparison with most of the others, the first strikes the ear as rather simple and transparent. Nothing at all seems to be hidden. Of the sixty-six total bars, only seven contain a third voice. Otherwise this story is told by a nearly solitary singer. It is the soul of simplicity. When Liszt referred to the charm and naivete of the Nocturnes, Number One could have been his poster child.

That said, the story that Field is weaving here can be misunderstood only by ignoring numerous signs that lead us in another direction. Following is a story that I hope will be helpful:

I have been given the gift of song, but there are moments, such as this, when it is not enough. I find myself lonely and adrift. Instead of exulting in what is, I lament over what is missing. Oh, I am able to renew the rush that follows a demonstration of my artistic skills, and take some comfort from that. But when I come down, I am always reminded that it is not enough. So the cycle continues. As a poet I have no choice but to continue spinning my particular magic as gracefully and enchantingly as I can. It is often a struggle to ago on, to continue reaching the heights with my song. I confess that sometimes I am smiling through my tears. And that is when I must remind myself that as long as I can sing, the song is who I am.

Let us examine some of the major elements of this Nocturne.

Of primary importance is the tempo. I would like to address this first because the Molto Moderato which Field posted at the start is the only legitimate excuse that the Liszt-Irish school has for misinterpreting this piece. The metronome setting for moderato is generally considered to be from around MM quarter note=88 to quarter note=104. At the lower end it is just above andante, and at the upper end just below allegretto. Thus, Field is guiding us to the lower setting, 88. Let us give the composer some leeway and call it 84.

This Nocturne is in 12/8 meter. For convenience, I convert it to 4/4 and assume four triplets to the bar, which changes nothing. Play six or eight bars at quarter note=84. Do you hear radiant happiness? Perhaps meaningless gibberish? Good sense has prevailed and the pianists who have recorded the Nocturnes agree. They perform Number One at MM quarter note=63-66, which is in the adagio range, not even andante. This is not surprising, because Number One is an adagio, for the reasons explored in Chapters Two and Three.

We can only speculate about the interesting question of why Field chose to post Molto Moderato rather than Adagio, or whether this was Liszt's editorial decision and not Field's. If this was the composer's choice, and he was being consistent from the start in concealing his debt to Beethoven, he may have avoided the adagio designation out of fear that it would lead musicians back to the source. Several years passed before Field posted the first adagio, in Nocturne Number Four.

Once we get beyond the question of tempo, there are no good excuses for finding radiant happiness and/or overflowing felicity in this music. Notice the *mezzo voce* right at the start. It is an important element in the drama, which begins in a subdued and tentative manner, as though the poet must first test his voice before declaring himself openly. By bar 6 he is more assertive with his leap of nearly an octave to high C. While this note is not accented, it is marked *tenuto*. It must be delayed, and the forward movement of the song must falter for just a moment. Early on, the poet/singer tells us that this is more than a lovely, joyful song. This is a story of longing and aspiration.

Another obvious clue is the preponderance of drooping phrases, motif #2, and the tendency of the melodic line to descend. For every bar in which the melody leaps to a high note, there are two or three in which it descends. During the first half of this Nocturne, instead of the soaring flight of 16th or 32nd notes that we find in some of the later ones, we have a leap upward of five or six steps, or a laborious climb to high C.

For the Liszt-Irish school, apparently it is no problem to overlook bar 27, which starkly expresses the opposite of radiant happiness. Here we find a *ritardando,* a major slowing of the tempo, with heavily accented notes ominously descending the scale to a low F, two octaves below middle C, and an F-minor broken chord laden with melancholy. Anyone seeking the heart of this Nocturne must take heed.

Another sign is the brief *scherzando,* bars 15-19. This instruction to hasten the tempo and alter the mood is uniformly ignored in the recording I have heard. The significance is that here we have the one moment of youthful exuberance, perhaps even hope, and its rapid passing serves to throw the rest of the Nocturne into a contrasting shadow.

Yet another sign is the constant juxtaposition of opposites. For example, after the flight of 16ths in bars 47-48, the lower voice drops to G two octaves below middle C, and a sequence of sighs resumes in bars 50-55. In bar 58, the sighing is in the form of triplets that descend chromatically, beat by beat. This is followed by a flight of 16ths up to G above high C. After this, in bar 60, the drooping triplets are repeated exactly, telling us that in this story nothing changes; release from our anguish is transitory, an illusion.

In summation, there appears to be a nearly universal refusal to believe that Field has a deeper story to tell, or that he actually expected the pianist to recognize and respond to the dynamics and verbal instructions in his music.

The disregarding of the *tenuto* in bar 6 touches upon a major tenet in the performance of these Nocturnes. They cannot, they must not be performed in strict meter. There are many moments, other than the obvious *ritardando* or *rallentando,* that demand an abandonment of meter, or at least a bending of the rhythm, often where there is no specific directive to do so. Contemporary accounts uniformly describe the principal character of Field's playing as highly expressive, even poetic. Why would this not include the performance of his own music?

Now let us consider a number of details involving interpretation and performance of this Nocturne.

The accented A-flat below middle C in bar 6 leads us to question the generally held belief that all the important business of the Nocturnes is carried out in the treble, the bass merely lending support. On the contrary, the lower voices play a vital role in the unfolding of the drama. In Nocturne Number One this role begins in the first bar. Notice that the first bass note in each of the first eight bars is marked staccato. I interpret this as a slight accent, accomplished with the weight of the hand, rather than a striking of the key. Aesthetically, these notes provide a satisfying balance to the upper voice. As part of the drama, they form a subtle duet with the alter ego, reminding the poet that, with all his striving and aspirations, he is still earthbound. The accent on the A-flat in bar 6 acts as a counterbalance to the first high C, an ironic reminder, at the outset, that the poet must not expect too much.

In bars 8-14 there are several accented notes that lead us far from the radiant happiness of F. Liszt. The sigh, motif #2, makes its first appearance in bar 8 and is followed by four additional sighs. The accent on the first note of the downward phrase suggests a sob, which is a stronger version of this motif. The poet's little journey, his brief flight to the upper regions has barely begun, and already he despairs. The accents should be given full expression by sonority and partly by a *sostenuto*. About half of the accents in this passage are suspended passing tones that set up in the listener a desire for resolution. The sighing phrases that contain a passing tone are a combination of motifs #2 and 8, a potent factor in telling the Introspective story.

Another component of the underlying melancholy is the presence of motif #6. Twice within the first section, A-flat passes through A-flat minor to the dominant B-flat. This shift of modality from major to minor and sometimes diminished chords conveys the fragility of emotions that pass so easily from melancholy to hope, from pain to joy. Whenever the harmony plays such a prominent role, a slight *sostenuto* is desirable so that it is not lost to the ear.

Bars 10 and 11 present a combination of motifs #1 and 2, a yearning phrase that ends in a sigh. In later Nocturnes, a sequence of yearning phrases almost always crescendos to the high note and then diminishes. That seems to be called for here. The crescendo from *pianissimo* should not exceed a *mezzo piano* at the peak. At the same time, the first bass note of bars 9 through 14 should continue to be marked staccato. This bass counter-voice is an essential character of the opening section.

In bar 15, the *scherzando* passage would begin *pianissimo* if one strictly followed the dynamic markings of this edition, with the result that in bar 18, marked *diminuendo*, one would be playing bar 19 triple *piano*. Please! Begin the *scherzando piano,* and diminish to *pianissimo*. Within the context of the drama, it is an expression of youthful exuberance, perhaps optimism, and it should be performed at a somewhat faster tempo. The *ritardando* in bar 19 supports this interpretation.

This brief passage leads to an outburst, *forte*, in bar 20, where the *mezzo voce* ends.

The ambiguities and omissions already mentioned are just a foreshadowing of what is to come. Throughout, there are dynamic and interpretive details that should have been clarified by Liszt during the editing process. However, so much has transpired since he assembled the first edition, errors may have crept in subsequently. In any event, the pianist who intends to perform these works will be obliged to enter these corrections in his copy of the score.

The *forte* F, bar 20, is a kind of launching pad and is repeated twice more before the leap to the E-flat above high C. This brief achievement is followed by a slow descent in sighs and struggle and more sighs. The repeated F in bar 24 leads in small, painful steps up to high C and then down again. All of this drama must be clearly articulated by the pianist.

Beginning in bar 20, there are more questionable dynamics. A serious omission in this bar is the *piano* following the *forte*. In every Nocturne that contains such a passage, the *forte* is motif #3, a brief outburst followed by calm. An example is in bar 35 of this Nocturne. If one were to follow the markings as given, the crescendo in bar 21 would be *fortissimo*, an impossibility. And bars 22-27 would be played *forte*, also unacceptable within the context of this drama.

The *ritardando,* such as in bars 27 and 33, should not be slighted and treated as temporary distractions. They are not marked *poco rit.*, but are full *ritardandos* that function as an anti-climax in the drama. They suggest that the poet may be exhausted and has lost his will, particularly in bar 27 with its accented bass notes descending.

Instead of resolving into the dominant B-flat as previously, at bar 28 the melody slips briefly into F minor on the way back to B-flat. Emotions shift uneasily from hope to despair and back, projecting a constant struggle for fulfillment. Another *ritardando,* another single note, *forte,* launches another leap of nearly an octave, until we arrive at bar 36, where a leap from E-flat to E-flat above high C results in the poet's first modest flight in triplets, beginning with A-flat above high C.

The first E-flat in bar 36 should have been marked *forte.* Without it the entire passage makes no sense. As marked, the piano in bar 35 would diminish to *pianissimo* in bar 38, which is not consistent with what is happening in the drama at this point. I repeat the contrasting *forte* and *piano* in bar 35 by playing the high E in bar 36 *piano,* making a brief crescendo up to the high A-flat in bar 37, and diminishing to *piano* in bar 38.

Bar 39 is marked crescendo, which apparently continues to build until the middle of bar 41, where the *diminuendo* begins. In order to avoid an inappropriate *fortissimo,* this crescendo must build slowly, coming to a peak, *forte,* just before the *diminuendo* in bar 41.

Bars 39 and 40 are unique in this Nocturne. Apparently this first modest flight in triplets is being savored, with three voices gliding on each beat from one chord to another: F7, A-flat dim., B-flat7, E-flat, G-flat7, F7, F dim., C minor, F minor, F dim., and finally back to the tonic and dominant of the key. Before this rare interlude is done, we have four-part harmony, a single triplet in duration. In these two bars, special attention should be given to the bass notes, which descend chromatically from A to F. A *sostenuto* in bar 40 would allow the ear to catch the shifting harmony with its emotional freight.

After another, much lower flight of triplets, the song returns to its simple origins. The listener is apt to feel that the singer has found some measure of contentment and satisfaction, and the end is near. We hear a sequence of descending notes, *diminuendo* in bar 46, and then the poet sends his song leaping up to E-flat above high C. Persistence is rewarded with the first extended flight of 16th notes that float gently down, waft up again, and then down. This is the effortless floating above the gravity of earth for which the poet/singer has been yearning and struggling.

But, true to the character of the Introspective Nocturne, the moment of triumph is brief, much shorter than the Wright brothers' test flight at Kitty Hawk. Accented sighs and sobs return in bars 50-55, with the lightly accented notes in the bass. The crescendo beginning in bar 54 should rise to no more than *piano* in bar 55. The next flight of 16ths on the third and fourth beats should be rather quiet and subdued, leading to a passage of six bars, 58-63, in which despair, struggle and renewed flights repeatedly take turns.

The triplet figure in bars 58 and 60 is an interesting example of blended motifs, sigh and struggle. Although they move downward chromatically, there is emotional effort and labor here. They reverse themselves and rise in bar 59 but inevitably return. Chromatics as well as major and minor seconds contribute to the drama, which is an acknowledgement of the cyclical nature of the poet's life, and the inevitability of loss.

Emotions are running high precisely because of the constant rise and fall of the action. Lightly stress the bass notes, particularly when descending chromatically, and consider a judicious use of *sostenuto* for the high C in bar 56, and the high D-flat in bar 63. The 16th notes in bar 59 should be played *espressivo*. Certainly avoid any strict adherence to meter that would reduce the final dozen bars to a pointless, repetitive recital.

As he often does, Field concludes this confessional night piece with a surprise, the only *sforzando* in this Nocturne, on a B-flat high above high C. This is the defiant gesture of one who refuses to concede, so don't coddle that note. Strike it, make it ring out, and then descend quietly in a graceful, flowing run of 32nd notes. Reserve a little *ritardando* for the final bar.

The reader may be thinking that the *sforzando* gives credence to Liszt's interpretation of this Nocturne, which seems to end on a note of triumph, exulation and joy. I understand that, ultimately, music is experienced subjectively, primarily on an emotional level. Two highly sensitive and knowledgeable critics can, and quite often do, find very different qualities in the same piece of music. If the reader, after all, prefers to interpret this Nocturne as a simple, perhaps joyful song, his task will be much easier. Projecting the complex dialogue that Field has been conducting with himself is much more difficult. That is why these Introspective Nocturnes, despite the simplicity of their surface and the loveliness of their melodies, present a challenge to the interpreter.

Before we conclude, the matter of pedaling has to be addressed. Because the piano on which Field composed and performed was much less sonorous than the modern grand, more frequent changes of pedal are required to prevent a blurring of effect and the smothering of the upper voice.

In bars 4-5 there is no justification for omitting pedals on the first beat. Pedal should also be applied in bar 8. The absence of pedal for the fourth triplet in bar 9 leaves these notes exposed and naked, and alters the texture of the melodic line. The pedal should be changed on the third triplet in bars 10 and 11. This passage is *pianissimo*, and the additional pedal prevents the volume from building up. Treat bar 13 the same as 9. Because a *diminuendo* is in effect in bar 14, apply pedal on the second and fourth triplets. Add pedals on the fourth triplet of bar 15, and the third triplet of bars 16, 17 and 18. This will allow the *scherzando* passage to sparkle even more.

In the next section, add pedals on the third triplet of bars 21-32. Pedal every triplet in bar 33. Less resonance suits the flagging of energy and the *diminuendo*. Add a pedal on the third triplet of bar 34. In order to cut off the resonance of the *forte* notes in bars 35 and 36 and create a more dramatic effect, apply a pedal on the second triplet. In bar 46, where the triplets descend staccato and *diminuendo,* a better effect would be produced by pedals on the third and fourth triplets. In bars 47 and 48, you can put more sparkle into the 16ths by pedaling each triplet.

In order to avoid excessive resonance, add pedals on the third triplet of bars 49, 50, 52, 53, 54, 56, 57 and 61. Treat bar 51 the same as 9 and 13. Add pedals on the third and fourth triplets of bar 55, and on the second, third and fourth triplets of bars 58 and 60. Pedal every triplet in bars 62-64. And finally, apply *una corda* at the onset of the triple *piano.* There probably will be some variations among pianists in the performance of the final three bars. Your sense of the story and emotional response will be the determining factors. And that may change from one performance to another.

CHAPTER SIX:

NOCTURNE NO. 2

In his analysis of the eighteen Nocturnes, Liszt compared the second to the first by describing it as having "darker tints," like "daylight on a shady avenue." Mr. Piggot says of this Nocturne, "Field sings in sad, lovelorn tones, but otherwise the piece closely resembles its predecessor . . . the same simple design."

Actually, in the second Nocturne Field makes a significant advance, far beyond the application of darker hues. The emotion he taps is deeper, and its exposure is virtually naked. I offer the following story:

I am singing, but as you can hear, this is a melancholy song because I am unfulfilled. I dream and yearn, while my sensible self constantly reminds me to keep grounded because what I want is unattainable. I try to convince myself otherwise by singing higher and louder, and demonstrating that I can take the heights with a brilliant gesture that no one can ignore. Yes, there are times when I realize that gestures and demonstrations are useless, they change nothing. But I am of two minds. I am driven and refuse to forsake my dream. So I re-exert my will and sing higher and with greater desperation—only to come close to tears in the knowledge that my sensible self has it right. But what else can I do? So I continue to sing, to console myself, to demonstrate that perhaps the song is enough, my skill and dexterity are enough, *bel canto* is enough. But I must tell you it is exhausting, painful and emotionally draining. Do you know what it is like to yearn for something that is, after all, a dream? It is heartbreaking! Listen to my sobbing and you will understand. Listen! Listen! I am more than my song.

The first clue to understanding this story is the Moderato e molto espressivo posted at the head. Field could have asked for Andante cantabile e espressivo;

but moderato and molto espressivo are incompatible, even mutually exclusive. Any MM hovering around quarter note=90 cannot produce any music that is *extremely* expressive. Field's Moderato, as we learned in the previous chapter, covers a wide territory.

In the recordings that I have heard, the pianists usually perform the second Nocturne at MM 8th=72-76. My own preference is MM 8th=72, no faster. This is barely andante, and not a tempo that holds for more than three bars at a stretch. Number Two is one of those Nocturnes that will reveal itself only when performed in an improvisational style. Once you have established your starting tempo, abandon the metronome. How are we to perform this, or any other piece of music *"molto espressivo"* without considerable rhythmic flexibility, *sostenuto* on certain accents and crescendos, and taking a breath between certain phrases? A strict or nearly strict beat will not allow this, and it is not what Field wanted.

Once again, the story and the means of telling it appear to be deceptively simple, with both upper and lower voices in single notes. Actually, Field is employing three voices, since 8th notes double the first note of each triplet in 16ths, forming a third voice. To project this voice so that it plays its full part in the story, those notes must be held for their full value and given a little extra emphasis. They may be seen as the poet's alter ego and part of a subtle, running duet. The yearning begins immediately, with a motif #1 phrase that spans four bars, and the poet needs all the support he can get. This recital is intense from the start, and the *molto espressivo* comes into play with the accented B-flat in bar 3. The poet does not have to warm up to his subject, and neither should the pianist.

The second motif #1 does not have an accent but swells in bars 5-6, where a *sostenuto* is necessary, not even optional. Notice that in bars 7-17, the third voice disappears. There is nothing in the mood or structure of this passage that justifies the omission. If there were not so many errors of omission and commission in this edition, as well as a remarkable inconsistency in the editing, I would not question this. Consequently, I continue the pattern in the lower voice, especially since it is clearly needed at the crescendo in bars 10-11, 13-14, and at the *poco forte* in bar 16-17.

In bar 21, Field directs that the bass line be played *legato*. Since the lower voice has been consistently *legato* from the start, isn't this direction unnecessary? Not if you understand that Field wants to ensure that the listener hears this duet in which the lower voice, the sensible, grounded alter ego, descends chromatically, motif #8. His *"legato"* is just short of asking for cantabile, which would be excessive.

This enlarging of the duet concludes in bar 23 with an accented high B-flat and the bass voice plunging to a low B-flat in the balancing act that Field so often employs. The dialogue continues in an unexpected manner, bar 25, when the inner voice abandons the bass clef and springs upward an octave to join the singer in those sweet sixths that Chopin and other romantics loved. Here these three-note figures very much resemble the sighing that accompanies struggle and loss.

As he often does (review bars 46-47 in the first Nocturne), Field comes up with a surprise. After a lingering downward *diminuendo,* when you expect the singer to indulge in some dolorous sighing, an accented G in bar 37 launches a cascade of 32nd notes, motif #4, up in a crescendo to F above high C accented, the lower voice rising as well, pulled upward, yet providing balance in thirds, rather than single sustained notes. This is a big moment, risky but rewarding.

We return to a fragment of the theme in bar 41, a repeat of bar 15 with new harmony, suggesting that the poet has been altered by the experience. Emotion rises and falls repeatedly with yearning phrases and sighs, while the duet continues. Will the poet be content, or make another run at the heights? Field has another surprise for us. Without the preparation of a crescendo, the principal motif of the melody, four repeated notes, now in F minor instead of C minor, ring out *forte.* The middle voice again joins in the duet above, but instead of angelic sixths, we hear a fifth, a sixth and a fourth, peaking with an accented sigh. Darker tints? Lovelorn tones?

At bar 63 we again return to the principal theme, altered still further. This time it is in A-flat, and the harmonic structure quickly modulates through a sequence of major, minor and diminished chords, motif #6. While the melody returns, at moments, to the tonic C minor, the listener is left feeling adrift, insecure, and not reassured by the sobbing going on in the upper register. Crescendos and *ritardandos* wrack and bend the theme until we arrive at bar 73, marked *espressivo,* as though the poet were saying, "Oh, the pity of it all. Do you understand what I've had to endure?" The confession is concluded with a huge sigh, from high C to D, almost an octave below.

As so frequently happens in the Nocturnes, Field abruptly changes direction, yet in a manner that is convincing when one understands the story. In bar 75 we are stung by the only *sforzando* in the piece, slicing through the atmosphere like a bolt. After a brief lessening of tension, the poet takes off in a second flight of 32nd notes up to C above high C, a point that Field rarely reaches. Well, we are apt to think, he's done it twice. Now we can all relax.

Not yet. The emotions run too deep, the despair is too heavy. In one of Field's most dramatic and heartrending conclusions, we are thrust into a seven-bar passage of accented sobs climbing crescendo up to A-flat above high C. This passage is also marked *sospirando*, which informs us that we are to create the effect of heavy breathing, gasping, sobbing. In just the second Nocturne, Field comes out of the closet and admits that he does, indeed, cry in his music. Here the sobbing is most overt. It consists of a sequence of 21 two-note phrases, the second and third notes of a triplet. The first note of each phrase is accented, producing a syncopation that gives the sigh, or sob, a greater urgency. Rising and falling in a series of three crescendos and *diminuendos*, it is the ultimate expression of the poet's agony. In contrast to all the recordings I have heard that sprint through this passage, it must be performed *molto espressivo*.

There are several matters of editing and performance that need to be addressed, beginning with the *ritardando* in bar 67. We are instructed to retard for four bars, until we reach another *ritardando* in bar 71. Obviously the *a tempo* at bar 68 was omitted. The *ritardando* in bar 87 also presents a problem. A *ritardando* five bars long simply will not work. There are two possible solutions. One is to post a Meno Mosso at bar 98 and begin a *rallentando*. The other solution is an *a tempo* followed by a *poco a poco rallentando*. Whichever you choose, avoid dragging out the final passage.

In bars 6, 10 and 15, the third beat of each bar is left bare, so that in texture it is set apart from the rest of the bar. This effect is inconsistent with the mood that Field is creating. The reason for the omission may be the shift in harmony from C minor to G7 in bar 7, for example. In each of the cited bars, the third beat should be pedaled separately.

The total omission of pedal marks in bars 21, 22 and two beats of 23 is unwarranted. In bar 21, pedal each beat, catching the descending bass notes. Pedal twice in bar 22, and on the first beat in bar 23. Do the same in bars 31 and 32. In bars 37 and 38, pedal could be omitted if this were one of Chopin's delicate and dreamy nocturnes. But here the mood and the story are quite different, with a flight of 32nd notes that are carrying a considerable emotional weight. Pedal with each shift in harmony, on the first and third beats. With the return of the theme in bar 41, we find the same bare third beat, which should be treated as recommended earlier. In bars 54-55, and 66-67, pedal with each sustained bass note.

There are other instances in which pedal is indicated but its use is not allocated effectively, certainly not for the modern grand. In bar 77, the single pedal will work, but for the *diminuendo* in bar 78, pedal on the second and third beats for a better effect. In the *sospirando* passage, bars 81-87, a pedal on each beat would avoid a blurry effect and allow the rising accented notes to project distinctly. But you may prefer a building up of sonority, in which case simply follow the pedaling that is given. This is a distinctive and highly emotional passage that warrants some experimentation.

Another omission occurs in bar 71. The crescendo that began in bar 69 should peak in bar 71 with a *mezzo forte*. As marked in this edition, the crescendo would continue until the *sforzando* in bar 75, which is unacceptable.

CHAPTER SEVEN:
NOCTURNE NO. 3

The third Nocturne tells a story similar to the first two, but the cast is different. Field abandons the stark simplicity of two voices, with an occasional assist from a third or fourth, and employs polyphony, which he learned so well in his study of Bach. This presents the usual problem of constantly identifying the dominant voice and properly subordinating the others. This will be dealt with in detail later in this chapter.

The drama is in two parts. In the first part we hear the now familiar story of the poet yearning and aspiring toward the heights and experiencing considerable anguish over his limited success. A major difference here is the livelier tempo, which lends to the effort a touch of boyish optimism. There is also the consoling and supporting activity of the lower voices.

The second part is slower, and while the poet continues his quest, there is a sense of melancholy bordering on resignation. His efforts are repetitive and predictable as the anguish deepens. But at the end, one grand, spectacular climb to the heights somehow makes the effort worth the cost.

The motif of this story is a simple, step-wise movement within the A-flat scale, from tonic to dominant and back, shaping the four-bar yearning phrase. Repeatedly, at the end of the phrase we hear an extended sigh consisting of C, B-flat and A-flat. The contrast between the concerted effort of those supporting voices and the poet's meager achievement makes for a poignancy that has no other language.

Liszt describes Nocturnes Three and Six as bearing ". . . a pastoral quality; their melodies seem as of woven of the balmiest breezes, sighing warmly and moistly; they appear to reflect the changing shades that dye the vapors of dawn . . ." Etc. etc. Mr. Piggott describes the third Nocturne as ". . .

delightful . . . charming . . . the murmuring semitones . . . create a drowsy, honeyed atmosphere, more suggestive of an afternoon reverie in sun-dappled glades than the mysterious sounds of a summer night . . . it (the melody) could be the pensive humming of a distracted day-dreamer."

It is consistent with the Liszt-Irish school to find the stimulus for these Nocturnes outside the composer, in the natural world. We are to imagine evening vistas with their colors and gentle movement, but never distract ourselves by peering into that deep and secret pool of emotion that nourishes the creative impulse. If Field was depicting any scene, it was the nightscape of his own soul.

Every detail in every bar of this third Nocturne tells us that Field's subject was inner and invisible. From the outset, the long yearning phrases and the major and minor 2nds foretell a bitter-sweet story. In the second yearning phrase, bar 5, the minor 2nd occurs on a heavily accented note in a crescendo passage. And the melody rises chromatically with five successive notes, intensifying our awareness of the underlying angst. Throughout this eighteen-bar opening section, the poet cannot rise above E-flat, less than ten steps above middle C. The apex of the third yearning phrase occurs in bar 8, with the accent on E-flat. The accent and the *ritenuto* tell us to linger, as though the poet is already soul-weary.

A subdued duet has been going on since bar 1, with the third voice uttering a series of sighs. In bar 4, this lower voice abandons the sigh for three beats and rises as the melody descends for a brief duet. With the return of the theme at bar 9, the third voice takes on the 16th notes for three beats. This is the beginning of a fresh aspect of the ongoing duet, since the upper voice picks up the 16th-note figure before handing it back to the third voice.

In bar 10, the upper voice is supported in its efforts by an interval of a tenth, as though that might make a difference. But again we hear that extended sigh at the end of the phrase, C, B-flat, A-flat.

At bar 13 another climb begins, this time supported by three tenths in the upper voices, a big effort; and though the three fatal sighing notes are sounded, this time their descent is adorned with a figure that rises a third before it falls, rises and falls three times.

The poet is not placated by this pathetic gesture. We hear two cries of frustration and anguish in bar 18, followed by a pause. Yes, the poet goes on, but the yearning is intense in bar 19. With the *espressivo* instructing us to make what we can of those six notes in the melody as they descend sadly, wearily, this yearning phrase takes on special significance and power.

There is no pretense here as the poet bares his soul. He again makes the ascent, and again he rises no higher than that dominant E-flat. Perhaps as a way of compensating for his disappointment, he embellishes his song by picking up several of the swaying 16th notes from the inner voices.

After five more bars of yearning in the treble, sighs in the bass, at bar 25 the poet exerts even greater effort in his quest for release and flight. He begins a series of yearning phrases, two of which peak with *sforzandos* and the attainment of higher notes, a G, and several beats later a B-flat, followed by high C in passing on his way down again. This is surely progress. But will it suffice?

At a similar point in Nocturne Two, the singer takes flight, aspiration is rewarded. But in this third Nocturne, a *ritardando* in bar 28 modulates into the key of C minor. The Piu Moderato introduces the second part of the drama with a change of tempo and mood. But there is actually no key center here. The poet is adrift in a sea of chromatics, accented minor seconds, motif #6, *sforzando* foreign chords, motif #3, chromatics in octaves and the upper voice ascending chromatically, and accented, motif #7. Toward what? The reward of soaring away from ground level in a flurry of 32nd notes? No. Not this time.

When the poet emerges at the other end, he merely returns to his plangent melody in bar 34, his familiar climb from tonic to dominant, and the concluding sigh—C, B-flat, A-flat. The *a tempo* in bar 34 does not return us to the livelier beginning of the Nocturne but refers to the Piu Moderato six bars back. Singing this simple melody at a slower tempo, with rising and falling sonorities and heavy accents, endows it with a world-weariness and pathos it could not otherwise have. As struggle and resignation become melancholy partners, the poet seems to be consoling himself by singing his song to the accompaniment of triplet 16ths.

In the upper voice the motif remains constant; the essential elements of the story are unchanged. We hear the same yearning phrases, the sighs, the pang of minor seconds, another half-hearted struggle upward in bars 44-45. A huge yearning phrase that stretches over three bars, crescendo, hints at some reward, some temporary release. Instead, the melody descends in sighs.

Beginning in bar 58, we find an unusual blending of three motifs. From a *pianissmo* base we have a leap upward, motif #10, a sinking back, motif #2, and a gradual struggle upward, motif #7, requiring nine triplet repetitions, to F above high C. So small is the reward for all that effort, yearning and anguish. In this laborious ascent, there is no gleaming flight of 32nd notes.

For five bars, a duet with an inner voice offers little consolation. Instead, we hear those yearning chromatics and accented minor 2nds, and extended sighs in the treble, one in each of bars 62, 64 and 66. At this point the listener is apt to expect the story to come to a whimpering end. But Field, with his keen sense of drama, has one more surprise. In bar 67 the sighs are now sobs in the form of triads, heavy on the first note of the phrase, letting go on the second. Triplets in the bass rise and fall repeatedly. Soon they are joined by a similar figure in the treble for five beats until, in bar 69, we have an explosive arpeggio followed by the flight that should have taken off earlier.

But this is not a brilliant stream of 32nd notes. These are modest 16th notes, upper and lower voices rising not in tandem but syncopated, with deliberate effort as though wounded and struggling to be graceful and fluent. This duo rises to B-flat above high C and celebrates their achievement by nailing those three notes at the crest of the crescendo before returning to earth. It is a triumphant ending, earned by sheer will and persistence.

There is so much in this intensely emotional drama about the determination to sing one's song despite the pain and struggle, it boggles the mind to acknowledge that other trained ears hear a peaceful interlude on a summer day. There is no final arbiter to judge one interpretation truer or more acceptable than another. When in doubt, I come to my conclusions by the use of ever-expanding concentric circles: the individual passage, the specific Nocturne, the larger group of Nocturnes, the body of the composer's work, and finally the composer's life. Then I stir with a generous dose of musical intuition.

Fortunately, the third Nocturne has no MM indicator, all of which, to some extent are much too fast in this edition. The direction, Un poco allegretto, prompted me to settle on 8th note=104. At this tempo the music has a fairly lively movement but is not so fast that it hinders expressiveness. The metronome should be used only as a guide and should not be ticking away while you are practicing. A metronomic performance of these pieces is the kiss of death.

While Nocturne Three has a busy inner voice in the 16th notes, the melody must always sing out clearly above the others, in both loud and soft passages. Unless otherwise indicated by an accent or *sforzando*, for all notes other than the melody, try the following: keep fingers close to the key, weight suspended, and produce sound with a light pressure.

Except for an occasional short passage, at least four voices are working, and the melody is sometimes difficult to identify. It may slip into one of the inner voices, or become absorbed into a sequence of 16th notes that are part melody and part accompaniment. In forming those yearning phrases, the melody progresses almost exclusively in steps of a 2nd or a 3rd, up and down. This restrained movement set against the restless lower voices contributes to the pervasive aura of melancholy.

In the first eight bars, the melody is easily identified as the dotted quarters and the 8th notes. But in bars 9 and 11, the first 16th note of the fourth beat is a melody note and should be stressed. In bar 12, the first 16th notes of beats 4, 5 and 6 are melody. All similar figures should be treated in this fashion and sung out.

Starting at bar 23, the melodic line combines 8th and 16th notes in a sequence of motifs #1 and 2. This is a transitional passage to the Piu Moderato, bar 28. Until the *a tempo* at bar 34, consistently sing out the upper voice. At bar 34 we return to the opening melody.

In bar 50, the melody is in the first 16th note of beats 1, 3, 4, 5 and 6. In bar 52, the melody progresses in the first 16th of beats 3, 4, 5 and 6, and the first 16th in bar 53. Bars 55-56 are an extended duet, motif #9. In every bar, sing out the melody and subordinate the 16th notes. These duets, which appear often, are an important part of the drama.

Whenever the upper voice consists solely of 16ths, be alert for the melody in a middle or low voice. Examples can be found in bars 42, 45, 60, 63, and 65.

Despite the somewhat confident tempo at which this Nocturne begins, from the start there are indications of subterranean angst and doubt. Besides the yearning phrases, there are accented 2nds and chromatics that must be articulated in order to establish the mood. There are no really ominous signs in this emotional landscape until bar 18, where two *sforzandos* erupt. They signal a deepening of the mood and must be given their full weight and force.

The change in key and tempo in bar 28 is another significant turning point in this drama. That fragile boyish confidence has vanished, so the change in tempo must be discernible. I perform this section at MM 8th=88. In support of the drama, the *ritardandos* should be full and suspenseful. In bar 32 a slight *sostenuto* over the *sforzando* would be appropriate. Where the pianist's musical instinct and intuition suggest *sostenutos* on some of the lesser accents, they should be seriously considered.

In bars 29-33, as the mood grows darker, the lowest bass notes require extra emphasis. There are elements of the duet here, with the bass notes occasionally given accents that make them of equal importance to those in the upper voice.

The crescendo beginning in bar 38 requires special attention. As presented in this edition, the crescendo continues until the end of bar 41, where a *diminuendo* appears. If followed, we would find ourselves *fortissimo* in bar 41, which is unacceptable. There are two possible solutions. One is to peak at the *sforzando* in bar 39 and begin a gradual *diminuendo* to the end of bar 40. The other is to create two crescendos, one peaking at the *sforzando*, diminishing quickly, and then building again to the fifth beat of bar 40, followed by a *diminuendo*.

We find a similar situation beginning with bar 47. The *ritardando* in bar 46 is an appropriate transition to a *pianissimo* in bar 47, followed by a controlled crescendo peaking on the fourth beat of bar 49 and then gradually diminishing.

A passage that is even more egregiously lacking in musical sense begins in bar 55. Where does the *poco ritardando* end? And what follows? There is justification for a slower tempo in bars 56-57, allowing for maximum expressiveness up to the return of the 16th-note triplets in bar 58. But that would require a *rallentando,* not a *poco rit.* Another solution is to post *a tempo* in bar 56, which produces a less dramatic effect. I marked my score with a Meno Mosso above bar 56, and Tempo I at the second beat of bar 58.

Immediately after the *pianissimo* in bar 58, there is a missing crescendo, which should peak on the first beat of bar 59. Just to keep things in balance, the editor omitted the *decrescendo* in bar 63. But the mystery of the missing dynamics is not done. Another *decrescendo* is missing in bar 65. Here the crescendo should peak at the *sforzando*.

By starting bar 67 *pianissimo* and building the crescendo very gradually, you can achieve an explosive effect with the *sforzando* in bar 69. At the top of the final flight, an emphatic lingering on the three accented B-flats is justified within the context of this drama.

The pedal marks also require special attention. The absence of pedal in most bars appears to be sensible if the pianist intends to perform this Nocturne in the manner of the Liszt-Irish school. The reduced resonance creates a lighter, airier effect more compatible with flowers and bees on a balmy summer day. The pedal marks provided in bars 2, 4, 10 and 12 are designed solely to catch both notes of the tenths and sustain the melodic line. But if I have succeeded in convincing the reader that this piece is not a pleasant idyll, the pedal must play a much bigger role by being applied on the first and fourth beats of most of these bars.

One exception is in bar 8, where the *ritardando* calls for pedal on the fifth and sixth beats as well. Another exception is in bar 24, where the fifth and sixth beats work better without pedal. In the brief passage in C-sharp minor, each change in harmony would benefit by a pedal change. In bar 33, pedal with each beat of the *ritenuto*. Also, add an accent on the sixth beat; there is no justification for its having been omitted. The *piano* at the beginning of bar 34 is *subito*, not the end of an undesignated *diminuendo*. Field is a master manipulator, a skill he learned well from Beethoven. He will by turns lift the listener up and cast him down, soothe and stab.

In bar 56, also pedal on the fourth and sixth beats. In bar 57, pedal with each chord change. In bars 58-60, another lovely color can be achieved, like shafts of light gleaming through the clouds, by playing the upper voice dolce and pedaling on each triplet. On the last beat of bar 60, try pedaling the accented notes, rather than the repeat in the next bar, thus creating an echo effect. In bar 66, pedal on the first, second and fifth beats in order to avoid blurring the harmony.

In bar 67, to avoid excessive sonority, pedal the second, fourth and sixth beats. Pedal on the second beat of bar 68, along with the pedal already indicated on the fifth beat.

While holding the *forte* pedal in bar 71, add the *una corda*. This was not necessary on Field's piano, but it helps to create the hushed triple *piano* on the modern grand.

If this Nocturne is interpreted as the intensely personal drama that I believe it to be, it will stand alongside the most memorable short lyrical pieces of Schubert, Mendelssohn, Schumann, Chopin and Liszt.

CHAPTER EIGHT:

NOCTURNE NO. 4

The third and fourth Nocturnes are similar in structure: both project two distinctly different moods. In each, the opening mood is lighter, more buoyant and positive, although both are colored by an aura of melancholy. In both, the second mood is darker, and the melancholy deepens. But within this broad framework, the unfolding of the drama in each is distinctive and gripping. The poet tells his story:

I confess from the start, while I can still sing gloriously, the burden of those emotional highs and lows is taking its toll. Do you have any idea what it is like to keep yearning for the unattainable while struggling with my demons? Of course not. You just savor the song, and thrill to the brilliant passages that scale seemingly impossible heights. But none of it is as easy as it seems, and is accomplished only by determination and effort. At the same time, the song provides me with a solace that nothing can steal or diminish. Ah, the lovely vistas I have seen. But I have also journeyed through dark, unimaginable places that have tested my soul. Yet I survive, and may be stronger for the struggle and the pain. All of it, the dark and the light, inform my song, and by that I am rewarded.

In Nocturne Number Three, the melody moves among the four parts, and at times a duet emerges for a bar or two. In Nocturne Number Four, most of the story is told in two voices, with duets everywhere, and sometimes we have a soliloquy in which the upper voice converses with itself. The duet between the upper voice and the staccato bass notes begins immediately. For some odd reason, a *marcato* is posted in the bass of bar 5. Its object clearly is the staccato note. Why was it not posted in bar 1, where the staccato 16ths began? If only that one note in bar 5 is to be emphasized, an accent should have been placed above it. My answer to the mystery is that Field probably wanted all of the staccato notes to be stressed.

In the fourth Nocturne, the principal motif, and the chief source of the melancholic atmosphere, is the sigh. It appears in each of the first five bars. In the third bar it is part of an elaborate figure, each sigh beginning with an accent. The opening acquires some buoyancy from the unexpected leap of nearly an octave to A below high C in bar 5, followed by an affirmative run of 32nd notes aloft, circling high C.

Of course, we would not have an Introspective Nocturne if the sighs didn't return, and they do, quietly in bar 8 and more prominently in bar 9. In bar 11, we have accented two-note phrases rising in motif #7, as though nothing has been accomplished, nothing good has happened. But, as usual, Field has placed us on an emotional seesaw. Again, without warning, in bar 15 we have a leap from an accented tenth in the bass to a chord that spans more than two octaves, *sforzando,* followed by a descending run of 32nd notes. That chord, like a brilliant burst of fireworks, is as joyful and affirmative as Field ever gets in these Nocturnes.

But after the sky-art disappears, the sighing resumes. The event seems to have raised some questions, perhaps doubts. A new figure is introduced in bar 17, the bass gently rocking like a musical cradle that supports a solitary voice singing sweetly above. This is the first appearance of the soliloquy. The 8th notes in bar 17 rise, and in bar 18 they descend, once again presenting the opposite poles that are so pervasive a motif in these pieces. The positive voice engages in that long, brilliant run of triplet grace notes soaring to above high C and back.

In the following bar there is another expansive chord, this time spanning over three octaves and bursting with genuine urgency and aspiration. It brings us to a yearning phrase that crescendos to E above high C in a naked plea that is one of the most poignant and heart-rending moments in all the Nocturnes.

After this, the soliloquy resumes in the phrase that begins on the third beat of bar 23 and ends on the second beat of bar 24. The response can be heard in the first note of each triplet that completes the bar. Which side will prevail? We have to wait until bar 27 for our answer.

Near the end of Nocturne Number Two, we encountered a passage of nearly hysterical gasping. Here we are, after a *diminuendo, ritardando* and a double bar, facing *piangendo*—a directive to start crying. Is it possible that tears are to be shed in these sunny vistas of birds and bees? Yes, indeed. Field seems to be saying, "Just in case you haven't noticed and understood the depth of my pain, here it is in perfectly good Italian. Play these notes as though you are crying with me." The tonic A major is replaced by A minor, F minor, and C minor in a passage combining motifs #1, 2, 5, 6 and 10.

In bars 28-29, with eyes probably still tear-filled, the poet and his song climb briefly upward to high C and immediately down an octave via the C major scale. Nothing in the first three Nocturnes prepares us for the next twenty-two-bar passage. While the poet, with renewed passion, continues his song, the bass, in a steady sequence of six notes to the beat, first note of each accented, ascends the C major scale. Something dark and ominous is gathering strength in three voices: the upper melody, the staccato bass, and the 16th notes protruding just above middle C.

Beat by beat, the sinister bass notes rise only to G below middle C in bar 31, and only to F-sharp in bar 32; but they rise to a disturbing *sforzando*, followed by a *diminuendo*. There appears to be a relaxing of the tension, until the bass note returns to C below middle C in bar 34 and proceeds to climb again, this time in C minor. In bar 35 the poet can no longer ignore this surging, determined force and descends almost to middle C, singing a few defiant notes before being absorbed into the middle voice. This is the first time, and one of the very few times, in which the melodic line of a Nocturne disappears and becomes part of the accompaniment.

With the submergence of the singer and his song, the bass ascends in sustained notes, not merely staccato 16ths, again in C minor. In the following bar, 39, the upper voice reemerges and continues the ascent, but now in the scale of G. In bar 40 the lead goes back to the bass as the singer is submerged again. The sustained bass notes resume their ascent, now in the A scale.

This duet between contrary forces locked in a fateful struggle goes on while the harmonic sequence shifts repeatedly from major to minor, the volume swells and ebbs, and accented notes ring out like clarions. In bars 42 and 43, the powerful arpeggios in the bass are like a strong undertow threatening to drown all just when the poet's voice has been submerged again. The octaves descend to C-sharp, two octaves below middle C, which is almost the lowest point, by a half step, in the entire passage. The cumulative effect of all that has transpired in this fourteen-bar passage is a sense of turbulence, instability, powerlessness and—despite all of one's efforts—a temporary loss of the self.

In bar 44, another expansive chord, *sforzando*, this one spanning four octaves from the depths of C two octaves below middle C, launches another wave of sound. The solitary singer is missing and silent as octaves in the bass, dotted 8ths and 16ths, toll eerily, reminding us of the fateful closing passage in the Adagio of Beethoven's Opus 27 No. 2.

Bar 46 offers some hope in a plaintive little cry, a two-note phrase in the treble, just above the 16th notes that rise and fall and go nowhere. That little phrase, repeated five times, reminds me of the dove with the tiny branch in its mouth that told Noah that dry land was near. This is also the resumption of the soliloquy, the yes and no of the matter. The first two phrases rise with emphasis on the second note. The last three are pathetic sighs.

In bar 50 the song, once again released, rises in a sequence of yearning phrases that crescendo to a passionate and triumphant B above high C and then return, *diminuendo* and *rallentando,* to pick up the theme again. Despite the sighing motif in the theme, which is repeated exactly for thirteen bars, its reappearance is almost serene and comforting after the turbulence and struggle of the middle section. Soon the song takes flight in 32nd notes, again reaching the summit of B above high C, and gracefully returning. Despite the continued yearning and sighing, this flight is a victory of sorts.

After the thirteen-bar repetition of the theme, we have another grand gesture, an affirmation of the poet's belief in the power of his song. The bass voice leaps into the treble clef and joins the singer in a flight of 32nd notes in sixths, a crescendo up to G-sharp above high C, and down. It is a slow return in the scale of A, *morendo,* to the second theme, which first appeared in bar 17.

This theme is marked *dolce,* as previously, but this does not preclude another sequence of accented notes struggling upward, just as they did in bar 11. Then, in bar 70, we have a short flight upward followed by five aspiring triplets peaking at F-sharp above high C. A leap of an octave to A above high C in bar 71 is followed by four short, drooping phrases, *ritardando.* Since the return of the second theme, the lower voices have been rocking gently back and forth, providing the comfort of the familiar. It is a cyclical story of despair and hope, of struggle and resignation.

In the last bar, the lower voice again leaps into the treble clef, and during the final *rallentando,* ending in a triple *piano,* the lower voice lifts the song to A above high C. This is another of Field's surprises—a grand gesture delivered in a whisper. It is all about the song, the song that will lift the poet/singer to the heights.

This is the Nocturne that caused Patrick Piggott to recognize the emotional power and intensity in Field's music. It was too obvious to miss. He describes the middle section as ". . . surging and throbbing in ever increasing agitation." But this revelation did not lead him to reexamine the other Nocturnes for less overt effusions of emotion. He concludes: ". . . the passion of the middle section and its powerful climax are all unusual features in his work." In a sense this is true; but it is merely a matter of degree.

Field's model for this uncharacteristic passage can be found in the Adagio movement of Beethoven's Sonata Opus 22. Not only the passage in question but several other musical figures and motifs employed by Field can be found in the Opus 22 as well as in the other early and middle-period sonatas. For a detailed analysis, I refer the reader to Chapter Four.

There is an operatic quality to some of Field's Nocturnes. Obviously, he was influenced by song, both folk and contemporary. But operatic vocal passages sometimes make an appearance. For example, in bar 20, even at the leisurely tempo established at the start, performing eight 32nd notes to a beat at the close of this long phrase strips this passage of its emotional impact. When performed with nearly metronomic precision, the listener is gifted only with a glittering display of technique, rather than the spirit and mood of the music. The tempo should be delayed as the phrase reaches its dynamic peak on D-sharp above high C, and not return *a tempo* until the start of bar 21. This would be comparable to a *colla voce* (with the voice) instruction to the orchestra in an opera.

The intuitive involvement of the performer is an absolute necessity in arriving at an understanding of when these liberties should be taken, because Field does not always specify his intent in language. He may have assumed that the pianist who establishes an emotional connection with the music will make the necessary adjustments. By contrast, Beethoven took no such chances. Especially his middle and late-period sonatas are filled with dozens of specific verbal instructions.

Another example of an absent instruction is found in bar 22, which should have been marked *espressivo,* or *sostenuto*. If the pianist cannot sense the nearly heart-rending passion and project it as though he were a singer, he ought not to invest any further effort in this Nocturne.

Beginning with bar 27 and ending at the close of bar 29, the brief *piangendo* section should be played *molto espressivo*. It makes no musical sense to play it in strict meter or anything close to it. *Sostenuto* should be applied on the accented notes of the three sobs, and at the peak of the phrase, the first beat of 29. Failure to respond to the poetic character of this passage will drain it of all meaning.

By contrast, from bar 30 to bar 51, the tempo should be rather steady, with the emotion rising and falling in the melodic line and the ebb and flow of the dynamics. At this point, follow the voice from treble to bass and back again, always singing above those relentless 16ths. And please, resist following the example of pianists who rush this section. Pushing up the tempo generates plenty of excitement but obliterates the profound emotional power of this passage. It should be played at the starting tempo, no faster.

At bar 60, marked *espressivo,* take Field at his Italian word, emphasizing the sobs with a full *sostenuto,* and a *rubato* in the longer rising and falling phrases.

The suggestion given regarding the triplets in bar 20 applies to the 32nd notes in bar 59, but always sensitively and never to excess. These are highly subjective decisions, and your ear as well as your emotional response must be the guide. At bar 67, *dolce,* the tempo returns to a steady beat. However, in bar 69 the sequence of accented notes would be more effective *sostenuto.*

In bar 70, the delicate, high triplets played *piano* require separate pedaling to keep them as clear and bell-like as possible in a passage that is pure bliss. On Field's piano a single pedal probably worked quite well; but this, among several other passage throughout the Nocturnes, requires a different approach. In bar 71, the third and fourth beats of those gently descending phrases would provide a more effective transition with individual pedals. A *diminuendo* should have been indicated here, and its omission is a serious lapse. Also, in the same bar, the indicated *ritardando* has no apparent stopping point other than the final double bar. I suggest that at bar 72 a Meno Mosso be posted, and the dynamic *piano* entered below. Then the performer could begin a *poco a poco rallentando,* beginning with the third or fourth beat of that bar.

As usual, and particularly with music as emotionally rich as this, experimentation will be necessary until the pianist reaches a level of interpretation and performance that is fully satisfying.

CHAPTER NINE:

NOCTURNE NO. 5

In his essay, Liszt links Nocturne Number Five with Number One. Both, he says, are filled with ". . . a radiant happiness . . . overflowing felicity." Do we know of any composer, even among the greatest, who has equaled Field's accomplishment of expressing "radiant happiness" in a piece marked Lento Assai? Even the triplets that make their way chromatically up to E flat below high C are played *pianissimo*.

Mr. Piggott reveals that Number Five was originally titled "Serenade" and went through some alterations before it eventually emerged as a Nocturne. After adding an orchestral accompaniment, Field inserted the Serenade into his third concerto, which had no slow movement. Later it acquired an independent life as a Nocturne.

We cannot know Field's mood or circumstances when he wrote this music. Marked Cantabile, Lento Assai, it is probably the most enigmatic and misunderstood of the group. The Lento Assai directive is the slowest tempo of all eighteen Nocturnes. Lento is slower than adagio and not so slow as largo. Initially, there appears to be an incongruity in the instruction to sing out a lyrical piece very slowly. That puzzled and disturbed me for quite some time; but eventually, with a deeper understanding of all the Nocturnes, it made perfect sense.

I concluded that Field's determination to slow the tempo originated from his desire that this Nocturne not be performed as a simple, lovely song. The song that he heard and wanted to project was an utterance of the soul, a voice more profound than a mere melody.

Number Five has none of the urgency of the earlier Nocturnes. Except for two bars, its surface is mostly undisturbed. Thus, in keeping with the Liszt interpretation of the Nocturnes, the Peters and Kalmus editions livened up Number Five and diluted the aura of melancholy by replacing the Lento Assai with an Andantino or Andante. It also begins *mezzo forte,* rather than *piano.* Of course this totally transforms the music and corrupts Field's intent.

In Number Five we meet the poet/singer stripped of all show, all pretense, all that is not absolutely essential. He is a solitary actor on a bare stage, sometimes exposed by a diffuse light, sometimes by a stark, glaring light focused only on his figure. After the turbulent scenes that preceded this moment, the stillness is unearthly, and the figure barely moves as he begins his self-revelation.

We are not surprised when he begins with two long, yearning phrases. But at bar eight we suspect that there may be a dark side to this story, a hint of loneliness and heartbreak. Three sighs, two-note phrases that begin in the upper reaches, descend as though drooping under the weight of their burden. And other hints along the way sharpen our awareness of the emerging story. In bar 16, with little warning, we have a D-flat, a suspended chromatic passing tone, *sforzando.* Bursting out of that sweet melody, it strikes like a cry of the heart. The moment passes as quickly and quietly as it arrived, but it has served as a foreshadowing of the explosive bar 22.

The next point of interest is the four-bar passage, 18-21, consisting solely of triplets in a chorus of five voices, rather than the single upper and lower voices that have been telling this story. In the earlier stories, we expected an exuberant release after the yearning and the sighs. But here we have triplets beginning *pianissimo* at ground level and rising chromatically nine-and-a-half steps to E-flat. These are not soaring notes in an assured, gliding flight, but a delicate, painstaking climb, *portamento.*

There is another interesting feature of this modest passage. While the highest voice rises chromatically, the quartet below diligently repeats a B-flat chord, anchoring and restraining the flight. Then, in the second of the four bars, the two upper voices of the accompaniment switch to a different harmony, parts of a chord whose identity we can only guess. At the same time, the lower two notes are repeating the tonic and dominant of B-flat. This clash of harmonies creates a harsh combination of a minor and a major second. In bar 20 the harmony reverts to the B-flat chord, followed by a repetition of the clashing chords in bar 21.

We now have stronger evidence of considerable underlying pain, and that the attempts to rise above it are half-hearted, pathetic failures. But if we have any lingering doubts, the poet/singer is about to dispel them in bar 22 with that outburst of two *sforzando* arpeggios.

For quite some time I had a problem with those arpeggios. What was Field thinking—or feeling? What was his purpose? Not only are we unprepared for this outburst, the poet instantly resumes his lovely song as though nothing untoward had happened. And then, two bars later, he leaps up to a high C, accented. In all of the recordings of this Nocturne that I have heard, the interpreter softens the *sforzandos* to no more than a well-behaved *mezzo forte*. And I could sympathize with the impulse to believe that Field did not really mean to let the poet lose control in such an unseemly manner.

Now I understand that bar 22 is the key that unlocks the mystery around this Nocturne. It is a story that assimilates opposites. Pain and despair make their accommodation with acceptance and resignation. The pain is clearly articulated in those awkward and disquieting arpeggios. And the acceptance? In bar 24, the high C is an affirmation that the song still lives. But the moment is extremely brief, the voice is syncopated and a bit off balance on its way down, and there are only four 16th notes for display. Another brief moment appears five bars later, when eight independent 8th notes do a bit of high-flying against the steady triplets in the bass.

On the affirmative side, only four successive 16th notes gather at any point, not nearly a flight; and only once, in bar 31, do they manage to rise above high C. That is it, the poet seems to be saying, the truth, the whole truth and nothing but. It is the stark recognition of limitations.

The story returns to the rising triplets that first appeared in bars 18-21. This time a small burden is lifted, the light glows a little brighter when the chords that we heard in bars 19 and 21 become a unified E-flat diminished. One of the two seconds has been eliminated, but the B-flat will not budge, and the harsh minor second stabs nine times.

With a two-bar coda, the story ends quietly in the bass clef.

Following are some performance suggestions:

As usual, tempo is primary. Field wanted this Nocturne sung slowly, not andante. Converting the 12/8 meter to common time, with four triplets per bar, I start at MM quarter note=54. But I perform it with considerable rhythmic freedom, *sostenutos,* and a breath between most phrases. A steady classical beat merely trivializes a tender, poignant piece. The melodic line is the voice of John Field, so let it speak.

In bar 8 the accents on the sighing phrases call for an expressive *sostenuto,* as well as some increased sonority on the first note of each phrase. This is also true of the accented D in bar 14.

The treatment of the rising triplets in bars 18-21 and 38-41 is of extreme importance in the interpretation of this Nocturne. Do not play them in tempo, or hastened, as they are in some recordings. These passages should have been marked *espressivo*.

Bar 24 should also be played expressively, on the descent from the high C. Treat the phrases in bar 30 the same as in bar 8. Bar 31 is missing a *diminuendo*. Without it the entire dynamic range of the following passage flies out of control. This bar is similar to bar 16, where the *sforzando* is followed by a *diminuendo*. In the last two bars, do not be in a hurry to start the second phrase in bar 42, or the first phrase in bar 43. A slight pause before each would be appropriate and emotively affecting.

Although this Nocturne is better edited than most in the Schirmer edition, several changes and additions are recommended. Because of the increased sonority of modern pianos, pedal marks should be added as follows; on the first beat of bar 25; the seventh beat of bar 26; the first beat of bar 32; the seventh beat of bar 33; the first and seventh beats of bars 34 and 35; and the seventh beat of bar 37.

The top of the crescendo in bar 27 should have been marked *mezzo forte*. All of the crescendos in this Nocturne should rise no more than one dynamic level. Bars 38-41 are a repetition of bars 18-21 and should be played *portamento* as well. There is no justification for marking them differently. The internal evidence informs us that the only change Field wanted in this four-part passage is the harmony, with which I have already dealt. In this passage, one appropriate minor alteration would be a slight emphasis on the high E-flat of the third triplet in bars 39 and 41.

Despite its rather subdued demeanor, the fifth Nocturne is strangely compelling. Set against two outbursts, its tender restraint barely conceals deeper emotions that only require a dedicated interpreter to reveal.

CHAPTER TEN:

NOCTURNE NO. 6

While the sixth Nocturne is subtitled "Cradle Song," we can ignore the subtitle in our quest for a satisfying interpretation. The theme, with its repeated notes and small intervals, is indeed simple and child-like; but several features are inconsistent with lulling a child to sleep. For example, the crescendo up to a *forte* arpeggio in bar 16 is contra-indicated if the purpose is either to soothe the child or prevent it from awakening. When the melody drops to the bass clef in bars 16-18, the accented arpeggios are also not helpful. Even worse is the *poco agitato* passage, bars 19-20. Surely agitation and slumber are incompatible. The same can be said about the accented A's above high C in bar 38.

The first 35 bars are very much in the style of the Idyllic Nocturne. In the first 18 bars we find only motifs #6, 7 and 8, and they are subdued, unlike their dramatic use in the first four Nocturnes. Motif #5 makes its first appearance in bar 19, the change of mood dictated by the *poco agitato.* Motif #10 finally appears in bar 26 with the leap of an octave to F above high C.

The extensive and frequent passages of 32nd notes, actually one of every four bars in the first 35, are closer to melodic embellishment than true flights that usually follow motifs #1, 2 and 7. The theme begins in the upper register, close to high C, and little effort is required. So we find ourselves floating easily in the balmy atmosphere of an idyllic setting.

However, at bar 38 we are suddenly transported to the darker realms of the Introspective Nocturne. Here are the familiar repeated yearning phrases and sighs, but only for six bars. Just as suddenly we return to the child-like theme and the comforting flow of 32nd notes, delicately rising and falling. In bar 47 the broken octaves progressing so cautiously and gently upward are just too delicate to suggest struggle. Yes, we hear a little yearning, a touch of melancholy, but there is no struggle. The poet/singer is unbound and can go where he pleases.

If this is not truly a cradlesong and not purely an idyll, what are we to make of it? The sixth Nocturne stands mid-point between the Introspective and Idyllic forms. This becomes clear when we observe the evolution of the first five Nocturnes.

The first three are the purest Introspective Nocturnes that Field wrote. In them the yearning and melancholy are most overt and are only minimally alleviated and rewarded. In Number One, which is saturated with all ten motifs, we find only five bars with flights of 16th notes. Nocturne Two ends, after the second and last flight of 32nd notes, with a passage of gasping and sobbing phrases. Number Three begins somewhat hopefully but falls into a long section of struggle, despair, resignation, and a brief hard-won triumph at the end. Nocturne Four is also Introspective, but for the first time there is something like a balance between the dark, painful passages and the flights of 16th and 32nd notes that occupy a dozen of the 73 bars. With this Nocturne Field moves a step or two closer to the blended Introspective and Idyllic form. In Number Five we heard the first accommodation between the opposing emotional poles in these Nocturnes. The underlying angst is still there, but it is much more under control. The heights and depths have been modified and restrained.

With this perspective we can see that Field has taken a big step toward the Idyllic form. The fundamental motifs are here, but throughout we hear those repeated flights of 32nd notes soaring above the yearning, the sighing, and the pangs of loss and regret. To this point, Number Six is the most balanced blending of the two forms.

The poet's story:

Blessed are those rare moments of calm and tranquility. Then I am at ease and can take pleasure in song that lifts the spirit. At the same time, I am aware of the yearning that never ceases. I may close my eyes, but I know it is there, lurking in the shadows of my soul. So I pretend for a while and lose myself in the splendid pleasure of floating aloft. I know, even as I sing my soothing and tender song, joy will ever be mixed with sorrow.

Much of the introspective character of this Nocturne is in the lower voice. The rocking 16th notes, with their broken chords, create constantly shifting harmonies that will soon stray from the tonic and dominant. The first and fourth beats of bars 1-9 are a staccato F, the tonic in this piece. But when the harmony shifts from the tonic to the dominant C7, the F will not budge. It sounds an edgy interval of a second with the G. This gentle pang, motif #8, also occurs in bars 3 and 11, the latter in a four-bar passage with eight repeated F's in the bass.

Along with these moments of subtle tension, the harmony begins, in bar 6, to waver between the major and minor modes, motif #6. The surface is so peaceful that this undercurrent of vague melancholy and longing may go unnoticed. Not until bar 38 does this aspect of the Nocturne declare itself, and then only for six bars. One supposes that Field felt compelled to draw aside the veil and reveal his secret: this song, dear friend, is not about infants and cradles. Look elsewhere.

Several bars later we find another passage, bars 50-53, that wavers between major and minor modes. Some of Field's most seductive harmonies are in these four bars. It is difficult to avoid being affected by the G two octaves below middle C in bar 51. The slightly accented 7th in the B-flat7 chord adds a poignant, almost somber hue to the melody, which is slowly descending to its lowest point, other than the final two bars.

As a motif, repeated notes appear in much of Field's music. There are ten F's in succession in bars 44-48. In this Nocturne they contribute to the darker elements, the poet's half-concealed story of longing and loneliness.

The Andante Tranquillo posted at the start suggests an *andantino*, particularly with those *portamento* 8th notes. This melody makes its way deliberately, yet sweetly. Both the Peters and Kalmus editions take this Nocturne into an entirely different direction. They ask for Andante Cantabile, and start off *forte* in bar one! This is a full-throated song, not at all what Field wanted, since the nuances and underlying pathos would be lost. The other editions also eliminate the Poco Agitato and replace it with a straight-forward *forte*. This sort of editing does more than take liberties. It is an inexcusable bastardization of music that could no longer be defended by its creator.

I play this Nocturne at MM 8th=76, which does not drag but allows for all possible expressiveness. Once again, do not play the 32nd-note runs in strict tempo. They are not "decoration" but an extension of the melody. Apply *sostenuto* and *rubato* wherever your sense of the story dictates. And let the phrases breathe instead of marching from one to the next. This music should sound like an inspired improvisation.

Wherever the melody is in the upper voice, it must sing out clearly above the broken chords below. You might think of the melody as performed by a violin, the 16ths in the lower voice by a harp, and the staccato 16ths by a cello, pizzicato.

In bars 16-18, the roles are reversed. The 32nd notes in the upper voice are to be played uniformly *pianissimo* and without any accent. The score indicates that the melody in the lower voices is to be played *piano;* but it could be sung at between *mezzo piano* and *mezzo forte,* while the upper voice, played delicately, rather than brilliantly, sounds as though coming from a distance. The two voices should not be in competition or engaging in a duet, as I have heard in some recordings.

There are some brief passages in which the lower voice rises in a true duet with the melody. One such passage occurs in the last three beats of bar 22, where the harmony moves from D dim. to D-flat7, to the dominant C. Two bars later, a lovely sequence—B-flat dim., A minor, C7—accented and *poco ritardando,* should be shared equally by both upper and lower voices. And don't cheat the *ritardando.*

A *piu mosso* is recommended for the Poco Agitato passage. MM 8th=84 is effective here. I also use some rubato. The *agitato* should end with a *poco ritardando* on the fourth beat of bar 22 and *a tempo* in bar 23. The *fermata* over the 8th rest in bar 26 gives you latitude to pause and make the run of 32nd notes more dramatic. This is an operatic moment, so sing it expressively, with a *sostenuto* at the peak and on the descent. The *fermata* in bar 43 gives the pianist another opportunity to tell this story dramatically. Pause, and then give a full *ritardando.* Everything should appear to come to a stop, as though it is almost too much of an effort to go on. It can also be seen as a false ending, which was a staple of Field's repertoire.

The three A's in bar 38 are one of the emotional high points in this Nocturne and should be played *espressivo.* In another context they could be interpreted as conveying triumph and exultation. Here, followed by a passage containing motifs #1 and 2, those notes are a cry of longing and pain.

Those inspired harmonic progressions in bars 52 and 60-61 deserve a *sostenuto* to bring forth their full effect. Also, bring another crescendo into bar 52, peaking on the fourth beat. Bars 50-53 require a true duet between upper and lower voices in order to bring this passage into a fullness of expression. It is the tender and poignant heart of this Nocturne. In bar 52 there is also a bass line moving chromatically from E down to C that deserves extra attention. This applies as well to the next three bars in which the lowest voice vacillates between B-flat and A.

By giving the staccato notes in the lower voice a little extra emphasis, a lovely and moving duet runs throughout this Nocturne. In addition to the staccato 16ths in the bass, the lower voice, in a variation of motif #1, picks up the melody in bars 16-18, 34-45 and 62-65. At the third occurrence, the *pianissimo* in the treble is placed in between the staves, suggesting that both treble and bass voices are to be equal. This is misleading and not what Field intended. That melody must always come forward as an essential part of the ongoing duet.

Regarding technical matters, we still have a problem with missing pedal marks. When indicated, pedaling should be consistent. Why are there pedals on beats one and four in bar 1, and only one pedal in bars 2-4? In bars 9 and 10, the absence of pedal for beats 6, 7 and 8 is inconsistent with a similar passage in bars 24-25. Why in bars 17-19 are some groups of 32nd notes pedaled and others are not? Nothing in the harmonic structure or the emotional character of these passages warrants such a distinction. In bar 14 the Schirmer edition calls for a sustained pedal for the entire bar. This does not work well on our modern pianos. Lift the pedal before the triplets.

Even more puzzling is the total absence of pedal in bars 2-23, where two pedals per bar would serve to maintain the tonal texture and contribute to the *agitato*. This same observation about texture applies to bars 40-43. In bar 52 the editor omitted pedal possibly because of the frequent change in harmony. A more effective solution would be the use of pedal with each note of the melody, and an additional pedal on the first beat of bar 53.

Of equal concern is the prolonging of a pedal when two or more would be more effective. In bar 26 there appears to be an error of omission, that is, the failure to indicate lifting the pedal after the third beat. The long 32nd note run which follows may be played without pedal for a more delicate effect. If pedal is used, change it with each beat.

In bars 44-45 we have a repetition of bars 3-4, where one pedal is held for a bar-and-a-half. Pedal should be applied to each staccato bass note, beats one and four. In bar 56 the effect would be blurred and out of keeping with the mood if pedal were not applied on the fourth beat. In the following two bars, pedals applied on each of those repeated F's would work well. After a pedal on the fourth beat of bar 58, the interpreter may wish to create a different tonal effect in bars 59-61 by complying with the absence of pedal indicated in this edition. Then resume pedaling on the first and fourth beats of bars 62-64. In bar 65, pedal with each tonic chord for a more delicate effect. In bar 66 the *diminuendo* would be more effective with a pedal on beats 4, 5 and 6.

The pedaling of the last seven bars is puzzling. Why are some notes that are marked *portamento* and *pianissimo* pedaled, and others are not? Applying pedal on the first and fourth beats of these last bars would work beautifully. You might try *una corda* with the triple *piano*.

The treatment of some details depends on your approach to this particular Nocturne. If you prefer the cradlesong story, you would then flatten most of the dynamics, and soften the accents and crescendos or eliminate them. The most convenient course would be to follow the Peters or Kalmus editions. If you prefer to treat this as a Nocturne that combines the Introspective with the Idyllic, then you would give each dynamic mark its full due.

There may not be a baby in this cradle, but the evidence suggests that a melancholy John Field may be consoling and reassuring the child within. Regardless of your interpretive preference, the sixth Nocturne is a lyrical gem.

CHAPTER ELEVEN:

NOCTURNE NO. 7

Of all the Nocturnes in this collection the seventh was the most difficult for me to understand and appreciate. All of those 32nd note runs, and particularly the cute crossing of the left hand over the right in the rising passages, and the right over the left in the descending, struck me as Field's pandering to his adoring audiences. Even the passages marked *dolce* or *con tenerezza* seemed to be an attempt to pluck at the heartstrings, particularly of the young ladies. In sum, it struck me as a fairly charming but superficial example of the kind of music that Liszt believed (or said he believed) characterized all of Field's Nocturnes.

The first step in my journey toward the heart of this music was facilitated by Mr. Piggott's *The Life and Music of John Field.* He reveals that Number Seven began its existence as the first movement of a Divertissement for piano and strings. In its next incarnation, it appeared as a piano solo, the third of three Romances. Periodically Field returned to the piece in an attempt to improve its form. The final version was published in London in 1832. When Liszt assembled the second edition of Field's collected Nocturnes, he renamed it, and the former movement in a chamber work has been known ever since as a Nocturne.

That this music began as one instrument in an ensemble of five gave some insight in my attempt to uncover Field's intent, the story. His interest originally may have been the constructing of a piano part that would project itself brilliantly above the four strings. A melody in the upper register and several glittering displays of 32nd notes might well serve that purpose.

Something close to contempt gave way to respect, qualified by the conviction that Field was squandering his talent. But repeated hearings brought about the final revelation. Number Seven was an Idyllic Nocturne with subtle and delicate introspective motifs. Field had been moving in this direction, and now he had taken the final step.

Because the intense passion of the earlier Nocturnes is absent here, the introspective motifs may be overlooked. Without the *sforzandos* and stabbing, accented minor seconds keeping us on edge, the harmony in Number Seven may seem tame, even trite. But its connection with the first six can be heard whenever the earlier passion comes faintly into focus and then fades like a distant memory.

The idyllic character is apparent at the start. The opening bars are in the conventional tonic and dominant of the key. But the span of more than two octaves between the two voices creates an open, airy, free-floating effect. When the two voices meet, in bar 3, we are assured that this is a true duet, motif #9. In bar 4, both voices participate in an effortless run of two octaves, with a gentle landing on A below high C. This is a sort of celebration of freedom, of having arrived. Part of the ceremony is a repetition of the first four bars, ending with a rapid descent of two-and-a-half octaves, hand over hand.

The duet continues, demanding that both voices be of equal value. When the song becomes a quartet in bar 11, the introspective element is introduced; Number Seven becomes expressively richer, emotionally more complex. The first chromatic, an A-sharp, is introduced in the bass and answered with an A-sharp in bar 10; and in bar 11, chromatics are abloom in the bass, requiring that this inner voice be given sufficient weight.

We return to the expansiveness of the opening until the song abruptly stops with a dominant 7th arpeggio spanning three-and-a-half octaves, the 7th at the top. Conventional as this may be, the spaciousness creates a fresh harmonic effect. We come down with a little sigh, really a sigh of contentment, another breezy run of 32nd notes, and this idyllic interlude eases into the passage marked *con tenerezza*.

If we are to affirm that this Nocturne is more than a moonlit stroll, the passage from bar 17 to 24 must be played *espressivo*. Now in their gentler incarnation, we have the yearning phrases, the sigh, the slight struggle upward, the leap—four essential motifs of the Introspective Nocturne. The careful use of *sostenuto* and *rubato*, and attention to the chromatics, will be helpful in bringing out the emotional sub-plot in this story. But there is more nostalgia then true yearning here, and it can scarcely dispel or disturb the mood of playfulness, the shear pleasure of singing and soaring.

The emotional duality that haunts these Nocturnes finds a fresh form of expression in the Idyllic mode. When the poet starts taking himself too seriously in the two yearning phrases, bars 21 and 22, he immediately reverses himself with a sequence of playful, almost coy phrases, *dolce* and *sotto voce.* He seems to be saying, "It's not that bad. Sometimes I just get carried away." This same duality of yearning and denial occurs at bars 29-32, 49-53, and 58-61. It becomes the signature motif of this Nocturne.

The four accented C-sharps give some sense of urgency to this first extended flight of 32nd notes. But the subtle element of yearning only serves to make the flight more satisfying. There is no struggle; the song is never really in doubt. The descent, at the end of bar 25, is something new in the Nocturnes: a rapid passage in which 32nd notes are broken into tiny two-note phrases. My first impression was that Field was being cute and showing off. But repeated performances of this Nocturne were enlightening. These running passages are not mere ornamentation; they are an integral part of the story and must be expressively articulated. Those three short phrases are making a statement tinged with tenderness and even vulnerability, and they need a *sostenuto* touch, particularly as they lead up to three accented notes that must also be played *espressivo.*

Now the extremely important question of tempo needs to be addressed. This is the most improvisational of the Nocturnes, and one tempo throughout will not work. Recordings that I have heard vary considerably in this regard. The opening passage is performed as rapidly as MM 8th=120 and as slowly as 8th=84. They are not even in the same neighborhood. The range within the Nocturne is also wide: 104-120, and 84-96, with stops between.

The problem is that there are three distinct sections that return in a quasi-rondo from. For convenience of discussion, I identify the three as 1. theme, 2. *con tennerezza,* and 3. flight. The theme, bars 1-16, is the fastest. I play it at 8th=112 but am not suggesting that this is the "correct" tempo. The *con tenerezza* starting at bar 17 requires a slower tempo, which I start at 8th=92 but bend quite a bit. The third section, beginning at bar 25, requires the slowest tempo, which is also flexible. I start it at 8th=69.

At bar 29, the last four bars of the *con tenerezza* return, and I am back to 8th=92. Bar 34 leads back to flight and 8th=69. At bar 42 we have a four-bar transitional passage that brings us back to the *con tenerezza.* I play this musical bridge at 8th=76. After the eight-bar reprise, again at 8th=92, we return for the next four bars to flight, 8th=69. The final four bars of the Nocturne are a repetition of bars 21-24, 8th=92.

With regard to this liberal approach to tempo, a fair and valid question may be raised. If this Nocturne is based on a chamber work, minus the string parts, how dare I reinvent it as an improvisational piece? After all, classical chamber music by definition is a written-out collaboration among several instruments that play in unison.

Fortunately, all of Field's compositions for piano and strings have now been recorded. After listening to a rendition of the Divertissement No. 1 by Miceal O'Rourke and The London Mozart Players, any qualms about my interpretive approach have been banished. When the piano enters, following an introduction by the quartet, the strings fade into the background and provide a chordal accompaniment to what is really a piano solo and not a true chamber work. The strings easily follow every rhythmic and tempo change initiated by the pianist.

Consequently, the pianist should have no hesitancy in playing the extended passages of 32nd notes as freely as mini cadenzas. These are examples of the lighthearted displays so characteristic of the Idyllic Nocturne.

Throughout number seven, Field works with the same themes and sub-themes, the same mix of controlled urgency and joy, retelling his story with minor alterations. By giving careful attention to the dynamics, the story will remain fresh and worth repeating. It may be just this repetitiveness that drove Field to reworking it over the years and delaying its publication until quite late in his life. Perhaps, at the end, he became resigned to the idea that this was all the story he had to tell. While the *con tenerezza* passages invite us to make the most of the introspective motifs, this Nocturne is primarily an invitation to enjoy, to relish the pleasure of free flight, the lovely phrasing, the playful chromatics and other delicate details.

To achieve this, we must once again deal with the matter of pedaling. To create an effect that is as clean and transparent as possible, a number of pedals must be added to those in this edition. A single pedal spanning bars 1-2 and 5-6 would have been satisfactory on Field's piano, but not today. Pedal on the first and fourth beats of those bars and in every similar passage. The total absence of pedal in bars 9-12 is inexplicable. Apply pedal on the first and fourth beats of bars 9-11, and on the first beat of bar 12.

The *con tenerezza* also requires pedal on the first and fourth beats. In bar 20, Peters and Kalmus call for pedal on the first beat, but beats four through six are bare. This bar and the next can be interpreted as the first dramatic moment, with motifs #1 and 10 converging at least *mezzo forte* at the peak of the phrase. Thus, a pedal on the fourth and sixth beats of bar 20 will help to swell the crescendo. However, if the pianist's choice is to make less of this moment, eliminating those two pedals is an option.

The *leggiero* passage beginning on the fourth beat of bar 25 cannot be realized on our modern pianos with the indicated pedaling. Pedal again on the fifth beat. The sixth beat can be treated successfully in either of two ways. Eliminate pedal, allowing the three little phrases to come floating lightly down. Or apply pedal on each phrase and enhance the expressive effect of the *sostenuto*.

Bars 26 and 27 would be improved with pedals on the second, fifth and sixth beats. Bar 28 requires pedal on the second and third beats. In bars 29 and 30, add pedal on the fourth beat.

Because of the repetitive nature of this Nocturne, no further discourse on pedaling is necessary. However, there are some odd gaps in the dynamics. Most obviously in need of attention is bar 42. A literal interpretation of these instructions would require that the *pianissimo* in bar 41 diminish to a triple *piano*, which would further be diminished in bar 43. The missing dynamic mark in bar 42 went unnoticed and uncorrected in the Peters edition. Kalmus posts a *mezzo forte*, which is appropriate. Another peculiar omission can be found in bar 49, where a *diminuendo* should accompany the descending thirds.

The Schirmer edition directs us to perform the four bars, 25-28, *mezzo forte*, and then crescendo to—we assume—*forte* in the middle of bar 28. A *leggiero* passage played *forte* is not slated for success. There is a missing dynamic at the fourth beat of bar 25. Drop to *piano* there. In bar 26 gradually build a crescendo to *mezzo forte* on the sixth beat, and again drop to *piano* on the fourth beat of bar 27. A similar problem occurs at bar 54, where this passage is repeated. But the latter situation is even more troubling, since the *mezzo forte* in bar 54 remains unchanged until bar 60. The *leggiero* has also been omitted here. Considering the cyclical character of this Nocturne, we may assume that Field wanted the two passages to be treated alike.

Number Seven may lack the emotional depth and intensity of the earlier Nocturnes, but it is a lovely example of the Idyllic Nocturne with Introspective overtones. There can be immense satisfaction in performing it sensitively, with an understanding of its true character.

CHAPTER TWELVE:

NOCTURNE NO. 8

Along with Number Six, this is a transitional Nocturne, midway between the Introspective and Idyllic forms. Readers following in the Peters edition will find it identified as Number Nine. First published in 1816, it was composed when Field was at the height of his powers, before going into a decade-long decline around 1823. At first called a Romance, this piece finally became known as a Nocturne late in Field's life.

Number Eight is unique in one respect. The waltz-like accompaniment does not appear in any of the other Nocturnes. Also, the abrupt six-bar return to the more common broken, repetitive triad is an unexpected and effective moment. But this Nocturne has much in common with the adventurous harmonic sequences and expressive chromatics of Number Six.

Nocturnes Six, Seven and Eight exclude motif #3 and present most of the others in subtler, modified versions. The opening phrase of Number Eight is a good example. In this motif #1, the quality of yearning is softened by positioning the phrase close to high C, and limiting the intervals to seconds, thirds and a fourth. Motif #1 appears throughout in several variations, some consisting of two phrases, as in bars 6-7, and in three phrases, as in bars 14-16. Far fewer accents appear, and they are never biting. The nature of motif #4 changes when the run of 32nd notes does not follow a passage combining elements such as motifs #1, 2, 3, 7, 8 and 10. If there is little tension, struggle or effort, the flight more closely resembles a decorative extension of the melody. All of this is typical of the Idyllic Nocturne. But in Field's Nocturnes, the spirit of the introspective always hovers over the scene. Its presence on the most idyllic nights creates a richer and more interesting story, as it does in Nocturnes Number Seven and Eight.

One of the principal elements of Number Eight is the accompaniment. While it gently echoes the waltz, Field does not want this to become a celebratory occasion, carried away by a dance rhythm. So he posts a *"spianato"* after the Andante. Omit the pulsing accents and smooth it out, just let it flow. Thus an affecting tension is set up between the subdued bass figure and the restless, impulsive upper voice that takes a high C, crescendo, on the sixth beat of the first bar.

The poet settles down in bars 3 and 4, contenting himself with several rather static, repeated F's below high C. But this story unfolds with little delay. In bar 5, there is a crescendo of octave B-flats passing from E-flat through a B-flat9 to another B-flat octave in the tonic, *forte*. In the space of one bar, the melody swells from *piano* to *forte*. Is this a burst of joy too overwhelming to control? The Liszt-Irish school might insist that it is. But the question is not even raised in the Peters and Kalmus editions. This provocative dynamic contrast is eliminated by starting out in bar 1 with a *mezzo forte* replacing the *piano*. Peters even eliminates the *forte* in bar 6, possibly viewing it as an unseemly display of exuberance. Peters only has a crescendo to an indeterminate height.

I am making a point of this process for a good reason. At the heart of this story is the powerfully affecting contrast between the placid waltz-like accompaniment and the intensity and volatility of the upper voice. The surge from *piano* to *forte* in the space of six beats is a motif that occurs four times in sixty-one bars, and the fifth occurrence requires nine beats, or a bar-and-a-half. It is absolutely essential that the *forte* be executed with full sonority and not flattened as it is in all the recorded performances. The repeated surging and ebbing of powerful emotion is the story of this Nocturne. These phrases are motif #1 pushed up a notch, and they replace the absent motifs #3, 4 and 7.

Almost from the start, motif #6 makes the first of several appearances, passing from the dominant B-flat to C minor and then to F minor in bar 3. Just prior to the *forte* in bar 6, the dominant adds a 9th with its slightly abrasive interval of a 2nd, motif #8. In bar 8, the suspended F-sharp, accented, *poco ritardando*, is quite affecting.

After a passage of major chords, F minor again reappears in bar 19. This story becomes clearer, the melancholy more overt, in bar 24, where the thirds in the inner voices form a succession of minor chords which rise in a crescendo that is expanded by a *poco ritardando* before descending. This combination of two motifs, #1 and 8, yearning in chromatics, reminds us of the deep ache that characterized the earliest Nocturnes.

Motifs #5 and 6 merge in the passage marked *dolente,* where a wavering between major and minor modes indicates uncertainty and ambivalence. The poet seems to be saying, "Look, I'm dancing, but my heart aches for more." This duality is projected by the abrupt and extreme range in dynamics, and by the contrast between the clear, open major mode and the shadowed minor with its aching chromatics.

Another example of duality is found in bars 28-30. As the song works its way upward with some effort, the lower voice, octaves descending chromatically from low F to D-flat, is pulling in the opposite direction.

At bar 43, a new mood is introduced, motif #5. These six bars are an island of calm. Sung *dolce,* there is not a single accent in a passage that should be performed with simplicity. However, you may wish to try it *espressivo e poco sostentuo,* especially when the melody rises to E-flat above high C. But avoid excess. Performed sensitively, the sweet simplicity of this interlude can be quite moving. When the right hand crosses over to sound those low E-flats, it is as though the entire range of emotion is acknowledged and accepted. The poet is earthbound yet aspiring, and perhaps philosophical about it all. There is a touching modulation from the dominant B-flat, starting in bar 44, to the tonic E-flat in bar 47. Field wends his way through light and shadow and back to light—B-flat, E-flat, C minor, F minor, B-flat, E-flat—playing all the time with our emotions.

After six bars of reflection, the action stops in bar 49 on a tonic arpeggio, *fermata.* Then, with a sweet, delicate cascade of 32nd notes, the poet appears to be affirming life by returning to the dance and picking up his melody where he had left off. But the gentle rocking between E-flat and F minor continues. "Ah," the poet sighs near the conclusion of his story, "our lives are an inevitable mix of light and shadow, joy and sorrow."

It is an affecting story because it is so personal and so honest. Field shares some essential characteristics with Schubert in his short piano music. One parallel can be found in the compositions of Schubert that begin brightly, with a lovely, affirmative song, and then, without forewarning, the mood sinks into the darker world of a minor key, a slowing of the pulse, a sighing of the melodic line. Both composers, each for his own reasons, had a dark side so oppressive that it demanded expression along with their need to sing. They were two of the most personal and emotionally transparent of composers who also shared Beethoven as their spiritual father and fountainhead.

At the conclusion of this Nocturne, when we suspect that Field has finished exploring the harmonic possibilities and the return to E-flat in bar 59 will lead us directly home, he pulls a B diminished from the folds of his cloak. Like an exotic bird, those 32nd notes take to the sky for just one more brief flight and he is done. We are comfortably back home again in the modest, unpretentious dominant 7th and tonic, triple *piano*.

Turning to some technical and interpretive matters:

As suggested earlier, the accompaniment must be smooth and almost always unaccented. To assist in maintaining these qualities, pedal should be added on the fourth beat of those bars in which they are missing. Resisting a faux waltz bass also requires the avoidance of a steady, predictable beat. Always allow the upper voice the rhythmic flexibility to fully express itself.

The small crescendo in bar 29 applies to all of the voices. Emphasize the harmonic sequence that takes us from E-flat to E-flat minor. A similar moment occurs in bar 35, where the harmony in the lower voices should be projected.

In bars 34 and 35, the crescendo at the peak of the phrase could also appear in bar 37, peaking on high C, and in 38 and 39 on the high B-flat. Although not indicated by the editor, such a change would be entirely in keeping with the mood of this story.

The dynamic marks in bars 40 and 41 are perplexing. The crescendo indicated at the start of bar 40 has no culmination point and simply runs into another crescendo in bar 41. Neither the Peters nor the Kalmus edition takes notice of this. A possible alternative would be to retain the crescendo and place a *mezzo forte* under the high E-flat in bar 41, followed by a *diminuendo*. Here, as suggested in bars 28 and 29, a slight emphasis on the descending octaves should assist in telling this story.

When the waltz-like figure stops, not too much should be made of the alternate bass. Keep the left hand as even as possible and let the melody sing out sweetly, and a bit plaintively. Apply pedal on the first and fourth beats. The 32nd notes in bars 49 and 57 are marked *dolcissimo*, to be played not just sweetly but *very* sweetly. Shunning any further instructions, Field assumed (perhaps hoped) that the pianist would play these runs *espressivo*, perhaps with a *sostenuto* at the apex, or wherever the interpreter is moved to do so. The run in bar 49, marked *pianissimo*, would do well without pedal if performed in an even, *legato* manner. The run in bar 57 requires some assistance, with a pedal on each beat that increases the resonance without blurring the effect.

The Peters and Kalmus editions call for an Andantino, somewhat slower than the Andante Spianato of the Schirmer's. None of the editions suggests a MM. I perform it at MM 8th=108, with a slower tempo at the *dolente*, and a slight broadening of the tempo at the crescendos to *forte*, as in bars 6 and 15. If performed at a lively tempo, say 8th=116 or 120, this piece will sound too much like a waltz and consequently undermine the story. A too-slow tempo can be equally undesirable.

Nocturne Number Eight is one of Field's loveliest, a superb example of the blended Introspective and Idyllic forms, one of the jewels of this genre. But unless the pianist performs this Nocturne *espressivo,* and is not timid about fully rendering the dynamic range, from *pianissimo* to a true *forte,* this music will sink into the banality bin, which already holds a ton of pretty pieces.

CHAPTER THIRTEEN:

NOCTURNE NO. 9

For an odd assortment of reasons, Nocturne Nine (number Ten in the Peters edition) is the most fascinating of the entire set. From the beginning I have had strongly ambivalent feelings about it. On the one hand, I view it as a failure; and on the other, as capable of creating a powerful mood.

The obvious source of my problem was alluded to in Chapter Five. The structure, the cadence, the mood, the harmonies—everything but the main theme—are boldly appropriated from Beethoven's opening Adagio movement of his Opus 27 No. 2. The similarity has been noted by almost every John Field scholar or aficionado with whom I am acquainted.

What fascinates is the question of why Field behaved with such flagrant disregard for critical and public opinion, as well as the judgment of history. The record of his life includes his penchant for returning to his music years later and making changes even after publication. He surely was not, as Liszt contended, "a model of grace unconscious of itself, of melancholy artlessness."

Considering such deliberateness of purpose, Field must have been unblinkingly aware of the response his ninth Nocturne would elicit. There is also a paradox enclosed in this riddle. This blatant borrower from the most esteemed composer of the era spent much of his adult life concealing his debt to that same composer. This suggests, at the very least, a conflicted and troubled soul.

The first essential step in any attempt to get to the story of Number Nine is to divorce it from the Beethoven Adagio. They tell distinctly different stories. The Beethoven opus is an elegiac mourning over loss, with a brief attempt to rise above it. The opening figure, not quite a melody, begins below middle C and is underscored by octaves that descend ominously down to C-sharp two octaves below middle C. The theme proper begins a fifth above middle C and does not rise a tenth until bar 27. It repeatedly descends below middle C and rises only once to high C. The palette is dark and foreboding.

By contrast, the melody of Nocturne Nine begins on E, a tenth above middle C, and rises to high C by the third bar. Although in a minor key and marked *dolente*, the lower voices do not exert a downward pull. Only a dozen notes in the entire piece descend beyond C one octave below middle C. The palette, despite the diffuse aura of melancholy, fairly shimmers and glows in a soft light. There is obvious pleasure in the pure melodic line, and the flights of 16th and 32nd notes. I offer the following story:

There are those lonely hours when I turn for solace to that most intimate of friends, my song. For a few precious moments a weight is lifted and my spirit departs the shadows and floats freely in a shimmering light. But a tolling bell breaks the silence, and sadness, that familiar shade, obscures the moon. I sigh and sing, rise and fall, destined to be an intimate of both sadness and song.

When I could at last comprehend this music as entirely Field's, despite the borrowed elements, I understood that it is in the spirit of two earlier Nocturnes. With number Five it is a temporary respite from the struggle.

In a softer, modified form, almost all of the motifs are present: motif #1 in bars 1-2 and 3-4; motif #2 in bar 6; motif #3 in bar 25; motif #4 in bar 25; motif #6 in bars 4-6, 12-13, 19-24 and 27-28; motif #7 in bars 15-16; motif #8 in bars 5, 15, 16, 21, 24 and 36-37; motif #9 in bars 5-6, 18-19, 21-30 and 36; motif #10 in bar 20.

With this underpinning of the introspective, we have a melody that does not allow a melancholy mood to prevent it from sailing up to high C and beyond, without the wings of 32nd notes. However, as in Nocturne Five, a *sforzando* outburst reminds us that a pool of intense emotion lies below and can erupt at any time.

In common with several other Nocturnes, the choice of tempo will determine the general effect. Performed at any MM setting below quarter note=52, the mood will be rather solemn. At setting quarter note=54 or 56, the mood lightens a bit and we approach the realm of the Idyllic. This Nocturne would not be well served at any tempo above quarter note=56.

Regardless of the tempo selected, the rhythm must be flexible if this story is to be told with any degree of effectiveness. For example, in bar 11, the upper voice cannot be properly expressed without a *sostenuto*. The descending notes in bar 12, marked staccato, should be considered as part of the preceding phrase and treated as *portamento* and played *espressivo*.

To make any sense of the bar-and-a-half marked *sospirando* (heavy breathing or sighing), each phrase must be expanded *sostenuto* with the crescendo, which is actually another means of indicating a stressed note. The original tempo returns in bar 17.

Bars 24 and 25 can be treated similarly to bars 12 and 13. The descending notes marked *portamento* should be given the added emphasis of a slightly delayed tempo. Field marked it *dolce,* a clue that it should be played expressively, with a flexible rhythm. The long 16th note passages that bring the Nocturne up to the final sighs, bar 36, are marked *dolcissimo*, inviting considerable freedom, as well as a delicate touch.

The sustained notes in the bass require special attention. Most hands cannot strike a tenth, which is demanded in bars 12-16. In bar 12, the pedal will sustain the third beat. In bar 13, lifting the pedal will cut off the low C. The better choice is to sustain the C with the pedal, particularly when the 16th notes are in a crescendo. There is no other choice, since no human hand can hold the low C and also strike the A with the third finger.

The accompaniment plays a more active role here than in Beethoven's Adagio. Starting at bar 5, Field introduces a duet between the melody and the lowest voice, while the triplet 8^{ths} remain subordinate. The voices answer each other in bar 6, where the accented notes in each clef should be partially enhanced by a *sostenuto*. The duet returns in bars 22-30. In bar 25, all the voices participate in the *sforzando*.

Some of the dynamics are impossible. The crescendo in bar 8 apparently must build inexorably until the sudden appearance of the *pianissimo* in bar 12. I have marked the first twelve bars in the following manner: treating bars 1-2 and 3-4 as motifs #1, crescendo slightly up to the G in bar 1 and diminish. Crescendo to the A in bar 3 and diminish. At bar 8, begin a slow crescendo that peaks *mezzo forte* on the second beat of bar 10. Begin to diminish on the second beat of bar 11. I treat bar 19 as a motif #1, peak on the F-sharp and diminish to *piano* at the end of the phrase.

Both the Peters and Kalmus editions address Schirmer's deficiencies in the dynamics department, but not always satisfactorily. Kalmus does well in the first four bars by supporting the rise and fall of two yearning phrases. In this opening section, the Peters edition exactly follows Schirmer.

Regarding the problem that spans bars 8-12, both of the alternate editions fare less well. Peters begins the passage *piano* and calls for a crescendo beginning on the second beat of bar 8. Let us assume that the crescendo peaks *mezzo forte* on the accented A in bar 9. On the third beat of that bar, another crescendo begins. Does it start *mezzo forte,* where the previous crescendo ended? In which case it must rise to a forte in bar 10, which is totally out of character for this Nocturne. To eliminate any ambiguity, the editor should have placed a *piano* at the start of the crescendo in bar 10.

In this same passage, the Kalmus edition begins *mezzo forte,* rather than *piano,* and also crescendos on the accented high A. To a *forte?* Presumably so, and unacceptable.

The other problematic passage, bars 18-20, is handled more successfully in the alternate editions. Starting *piano,* the crescendo begins on the fourth beat of bar 18 and peaks on the third beat of bar 20, the dynamic undisclosed but evidently a *mezzo forte.* The *pianissimo* begins on the fourth beat, not on the third, as indicated, for some mysterious reason, in the Schirmer's. Peters and Kalmus agree that it belongs on the fourth beat where the repeated B's leap an octave and are heard as though from a distance.

Both Peters and Kalmus also agree, correctly, that the *ritardando* in bar 21 should begin on the first beat, rather than the third, as indicated in the Schirmer edition. Musically it makes much more sense to begin the *ritardando* where the melody drops nearly two full octaves to an accented note.

This entire discussion demonstrates, once again, that the pianist who desires to perform these Nocturnes at the highest possible level must, in effect, design his own edition. We can only hope that some day that work will be done by a highly knowledgeable editor.

There are other questions of pedaling that are identical to those addressed in previous chapters. Wherever you wish to control the resonance, as in bar 6, add pedal on the second and third beats. Peters also amends this bar, as well as several others, and is generally a good source of alternate pedaling for all the Nocturnes. When Schirmer omits a pedal where you are convinced one belongs, do not hesitate to add it. One example in the ninth Nocturne is in bars 18-19. There is no reason to discontinue use of pedal on the third and fourth beats of bar 18 and all of bar 19.

In bar 25, both the Peters and Kalmus editions correctly indicate pedal changes on each beat, rather than the single sustained pedal in Schirmer. In bar 31, in order to achieve the sweet, delicate effect that Field requests, the pedal should not be held for nearly two bars but rather applied anew with each beat of this long run, and then again on the third beat of bar 32. There is no reason why bars 33 and 34 would not be pedaled on each beat as well. You might also try these runs without any pedal and compare the effect. The final bar would be assisted by *una corda.*

Mr. Piggott is quite taken with this Nocturne. He admires Field's ability to compress so much intense emotion into such a small form. Of the figure in the bass he says: "The triplet accompaniment supporting the melody in this nocturne is of the utmost simplicity, yet it is exactly right for the tragic feeling contained in the melodic line. A more elaborate texture would have diminished the pathetic effect of the desolate theme." This is a perceptive critique of Field's good musical judgment. But Piggott should have added that Field recognized genius when he encountered it, and that he only needed Beethoven's Adagio to determine the accompanying figure. However, in passing, he does point out that bars 20 and 21 of this Nocturne are one passage ". . . on which the celebrated Adagio . . . seems to have left its mark."

Actually, the ninth Nocturne is more dramatic and anguished than Beethoven's Adagio, which is quite controlled, its melancholy so resigned that it resembles an elegy. While the Adagio has it accented notes, they are not the pangs of anguish that we find in the Nocturne, in bars 24-25 and 36-37.

Further comparison of the two works is fundamentally unproductive. The pianist would serve Field more effectively by blocking out what he knows and feels about the Beethoven opus. The Adagio may be the father, but the offspring is his own person. Of course, achieving such a disconnect is not easy. The opus 27 No. 2 is one of those works that are so powerful, they take root in the psyche, like very happy or quite dreadful childhood experiences.

The major obstacle in our approach to this Nocturne may be that, of all eighteen, it is the least original. Despite its obvious departures from Beethoven's Adagio, it lacks the inventiveness, the freshness, the element of surprise that we find in even the earliest of the Nocturnes. Some of these qualities appear briefly and subtly in the harmonic sequence in bars 22-23, and in the unusual accents in the final two bars.

Ultimately, if you believe the story of this Nocturne and can immerse yourself in it, an excellent performance will rescue it. And that is all that matters.

CHAPTER FOURTEEN:

NOCTURNE NO. 10

This Nocturne was originally conceived as a one-movement work for piano and strings with the title, "Grand Pastorale." Field later revised it, dropping the string parts and starting where the piano enters after a thirty-four bar introduction. He assigned it the title, "Nocturne Pastorale," and Liszt included it in his collection as a Nocturne. Readers following in the Peters edition will find it as Nocturne Seventeen.

At one point during the life of this piece, Field made a piano reduction of the string quartet introduction. He later dropped that section, but the Peters and Kalmus editions include it. John O'Conor recorded it with the introduction in a fine performance.

My first encounter with this Nocturne occurred when I possessed only the antique Schirmer edition, with the Andante Con Moto posted at the head. This is almost the fastest Andante, close to moderato, and my attempts at producing music that was even mildly expressive at that tempo were foiled.

Later, an examination of the Peters edition cast an entirely different light on the problem. Field's piano reduction of the string section is marked Lento; and when the main theme appears, no change of tempo is indicated. The Andante Con Moto is a fiction. Played at the original tempo, an entirely different piece of music emerges.

The thirty-four bar introduction is an atmospheric passage which has subtle, partially disguised variants of motifs #1 and 2, and several forthright occurrences of motifs #3 and 8. Beyond those features, it has nothing in common with any of the other Nocturnes. It simply serves an introductory function. That said, I am not dismissing these thirty-four bars as inferior or lacking in interest. To the contrary, this is a remarkably evocative passage that transcends romanticism and anticipates impressionism by about sixty years. Only eight bars contain a melody. Everything else establishes a mood for what follows.

Turning to the Peters edition, let us examine those thirty-four bars. The given MM of 8th=100 works well. We begin in a somewhat subdued *mezzo voce*, as in the first Nocturne. But here something has been added right at the start: the intermittent repeated note, sustained like a bell. We seem to be entering a secret, possibly holy place, and a ritual of some kind is about to begin. Reverentially, almost no movement takes place. The first seven bars are in the tonic, with the E being repeated and sustained five times. We also have a simple, restrained duet between the upper and lower voices. When the dominant B appears in bar 8, the effect is satisfying, yet accompanied by an air of anticipation. Two bars later we slip into the foreign territory of F-sharp minor, and the ritual bell tolls an F-sharp instead of E.

There follows a simple, brief transition, taken by a solo voice in the treble.

The entire middle section, with its chromatics and elusive, shifting harmonies, takes us on a mysterious journey. Adding to the diffusion of the harmonic center is Field's repetition of the F-sharp in the treble and the sustained dominant E in the middle voice. The E is repeated six times in the first three bars of this section, and once in each bar it rings out *sforzando*. This dynamic mark is placed between the clefs, but it should apply only to the E. Set against the repetitive chromatic figure in the treble, it is insistent, even passionate. The aura of mystery and foreboding is generated in the sub-dominant A, which also contributes to the diffusion of the key center.

Employing a triplet figure that either rises or falls, the mood builds hypnotically. In this passage there are subtle variations on the introspective motifs, such as the flattened yearning phrases with a *sforzando* at the center. In bars 19-21, the three-note phrases descend in a sequence of sighs. Set against the sighing, we hear a return to harmonic stability with tonic followed by dominant, repeated. When the yearning phrases return in bars 22-26, the harmony continues tonic and dominant, signaling some kind of resolution. At the same time, there is more tolling of sustained notes in the lowest voice.

In bar 27 an actual melody finally appears, a sequence that could have come from any of Field's previous Nocturnes. With eight bars of these sweetly flowing phrases, the introduction comes to a close.

The version in the Peters edition, starting at bar 35, is Field's original reduction of the quintet. After the composer shortened it by twenty-nine bars, it was published as it appears in the Schirmer edition. Hence, the reader will have to switch to Schirmer in order to follow my analysis. For this purpose, bar 35 will become bar 1.

During my early excursions through this section, I had no inkling of what story Field was trying to tell. The scales have since fallen from my eyes. Indeed, we seem to have entered some enchanted place. The mellow poet is at ease, singing a song that skips with a lighthearted lilt. He interrupts his song for a moment in bar 3 with a delicate, celebratory run of grace notes, up to high C. Even the *sforzando* chords in bars 6 and 7 erupt like joyous, almost mischievous outbursts. There is no yearning, no struggle, only the joy of singing freely; and for eight bars, 9-16, the 32nd notes go soaring as high as G two octaves above high C. Life can be good. Yet, there is some defiance in the *fortissimo* chord, bar 14, and the *sforzando* chord that reaches an impressive F-sharp above high C.

After this display, the poet turns rather sober. He leaps an octave in bar 19 but immediately returns in a modest run of 16th notes. In the ambivalent emotional life of these Nocturnes, abrupt changes of mood are common. But here Field prepares us with a ten-bar passage containing five motifs. In bar 22 the two-note phrases seem to be floating down from the upper regions. On the third beat of bar 23, the phrase becomes a sigh. In the next bar, two sighs begin with accented notes that sound like sobs, accompanied by the A, *sforzando*, in the middle voice. Undoubtedly we are being drawn to a shadowy place. In bars 25-26 we find a duet in which upper and lower voices console each other.

In the middle section, bars 31-47, we have traded E major for E-minor, and as that lovely melody tugs at your heart, you know it's confession time. Yes, the poet demonstrates by leaping way above high C, he can still sing, and with ease; but the yearning for more always lurks in the shadows. Somewhat burdened by this knowledge, after some effort the poet leaps decisively up to B above high C, claims it with a sharp accent that leaves nothing in doubt, and then descends gracefully in 32nds.

Now that the poet/singer has unburdened himself once again, the remainder of this Nocturne is a return to the joy of free flight, mixed, as always with those darker harmonies, the yearning and sighing. There is a brief pause for reflection in bar 62, and then the poet continues singing and sighing, doing what he was destined to do.

At the close of the Nocturne he puts on a good show, simple, elegant but dramatic. The story is all about the journey, and now it is done. This may be the loveliest example of Field's blending of the Introspective and Idyllic styles.

Now we turn to all those details that should result in an effective and compelling performance. In establishing the tempo, we must first ignore the Andante Con Moto posted in the Schirmer edition. The Lento MM 8th=100 in the Peters edition is better but still too fast for a Nocturne that has 32nd

note runs in more than half its 90 bars. Experimentation convinced me that this story should start no faster than $8^{th}=88$.

But in this improvisational piece the first deviation from the starting tempo occurs almost immediately, in bar 3. No attempt should be made to play those grace notes on one beat. A slight pause before starting the next phrase would also be appropriate. Since this is not a pure Idyll, articulate all the crescendos and *sforzandos*. In bar 8, the tiny *pianissimo* phrase is spiked by the E in an inner voice that forms a minor second, motif #8.

This Nocturne is extremely operatic in character, and the soloist enters at bar 9. The coloratura soprano has taken center stage, and the orchestra adjusts to the melodic line that she spins. This passage could be taken at $8^{th}=88$, but slightly slower it becomes more expressive and charming. Even at a slower tempo, liberties should be taken. One such point would be in bar 11, where the four 32nd notes to the beat become six. This will certainly apply to bar 13, especially because it is marked *con forza*, which calls for extra weight on each note. The last three bars of this passage should be played *molto espressivo*.

It would be appropriate to return to Tempo Primo in bar 17 and for the next six bars, but always with flexibility of phrasing, in a singing style. In this seven-bar passage there are elements of the Introspective blended with and modified by the Idyllic. There is the leap of an octave in bar 18; a duet in bar 20; a long yearning phrase that rises to E above high C in bar 21, followed by rather shallow sighs; and another motif #1 starting on the fourth beat of bar 23. This last should be played somewhat broadly, and return *a tempo* in the next bar.

Because the next seven bars, from 24 to 30, are a transition to the key of E minor, the introspective motifs need special attention. Motif #2 in bar 24 calls for a *sostenuto* especially because it is accompanied by that *sforzando* A. The passages in 32nd notes should be played expressively.

The dramatic effectiveness of this mood change at bar 31 would be diminished by a return to Tempo Primo. It pleads for a slower tempo, and I play it at $8^{th}=80$. The staccato bass notes should get some emphasis, particularly when they move chromatically. This passage is a good example of motif #6, with the constant movement from minor to major tonalities. The bass plays an important part in this passage by providing both a counter melody and rather affecting chromatics. In bar 34, something of unusual harmonic interest occurs. The chord is G major, and on the fourth beat it is highly altered, with a second and fourth replacing the third of the chord. Thus we have two major seconds, the gentle thrust of motif #8. This harmonic figure is repeated in bar 35.

In bars 36-37 Field summons up the repeated notes in the upper voice which figured so prominently in the thirty-four bar introduction. Only the first note of each set is accented. The others should be softer than the three-part melody in the bass. They are a variation of the yearning phrase made more poignant by the chromatics, and they should be played *espressivo*. This entire passage projects a mood of restlessly rising and falling emotion, with rapid chord changes in bars 28-29, and calm followed by agitation in bars 40-43. The crescendo beginning in bar 41 expands the emotional impact of this passage by building slowly and peaking to *forte* on the sharply accented B above high C and then descending through the tonic E minor to B.

Four bars are required to make the transition back to the original key and the main theme. Against simple harmonic changes in the bass from B to E minor and back to B, a repeated four-note chromatic figure in the treble constantly curls around itself, returning to the starting note twenty-three times in succession. The operatic quality, with its drawn out atmosphere of suspense, is totally appropriate to this moment in the drama. However, if this Nocturne is performed entirely in the temperate Idyllic style, these four bars will be just another string of notes.

The main theme does not return immediately with the change of key. First we have a stream of 32nd notes rising deliberately, in stages, to a lofty B above high C, the same note attained with such fervor in bar 43. Then the theme reemerges, but now sung by an inner voice that rings out *mezzo forte* while the upper voice floats above, *pianissimo*. This melody should be played expansively as though sung by a tenor who is hopelessly in love. In this lovely passage, chromatics mingle with diatonics. In bar 53 there is an affecting chromatic movement by two inner voices that rise from E/G-sharp to G-sharp/B. At this point the upper voice, no longer *pianissimo*, will crescendo as well.

At the conclusion of the theme, we are back to the introspective motifs. In bar 56 the sobbing phrases from bar 24 return slightly altered. The earlier two-note phrase is now a triplet, also accented on the first note. Apply *sostenuto* here. After a brief yearning phrase in the same bar, the original two-note motif #2 returns. And again we have the duet in 32nd notes, first the upper and then the lower voice, sung tenderly.

There are two ways to interpret bars 62-68, both acceptable. If you feel a need for greater contrast, return to Tempo Primo, MM 8th=88. If you want to draw out the aura of melancholy, stay with the slower tempo. If you select the faster tempo, the descending 32nds in bar 69 should be *poco ritardando*. The slower tempo will allow the yearning chromatic phrases in bars 69-70 to be expressed properly. The emotional ambivalence in the Nocturnes never ceases and constantly requires the sensitive response of the performer.

At the end of bar 73, a slight pause is called for before attacking the *forte* passage, which should be sung broadly and assertively until the *diminuendo* in bar 77. Any tendency to flatten the dynamic contrasts is contrary to the inherent character of Field's Nocturnes and should be resisted. If Liszt is correct, Field may have projected a persona of serene indifference, but his nature was profoundly passionate.

If the pianist maintains the slower tempo into bar 80, he may have the uncomfortable feeling that the story has come to a virtual standstill. But the moments of silence in these two bars can be quite effective. After the 32nd notes gracefully rise from the low B to the E in the treble, the bell motif returns. The delicate chiming of the high E seems to promise a fading away to the conclusion. But Field's love of the unexpected shows up again. Quite appropriately, considering the expansiveness of expression in this Nocturne, he has the lower and upper voice at opposite ends of the keyboard approaching each other *forte,* almost triumphantly. Field does this not once but three times, again employing repetition with telling effect. But make a note to enter the missing *diminuendo* on the fifth beat of bar 84.

The final descent of the 32nd notes, *diminuendo,* can be played in a variety of ways. Experiment until you feel satisfied. You may even vary this final passage depending upon your sense of the story at the time of performance. There are numerous interpretive questions and challenges in this Nocturne, and this passage is just one of them. You may never feel that you own this piece, but through it you will experience romantic expression at a very high level.

Several technical matters require attention. As usual, pedaling is one of them. The Schirmer edition has no pedal indicators in the first eight bars, possibly because the chords in the bass are detached. But they must be played as arpeggios, and catching each one with the pedal is necessary. In bar 3, after pedaling the fourth beat, release the pedal and allow the rapid notes to sparkle as they rise to high C. Pedal the first beat of bar 6 and release. Do the same in bar 7, but pedal with each chord in that phrase, which includes the first beat of bar 8.

In bars 11 and 12, wherever the 32nd notes are to be played *piano,* you can reduce the resonance and produce a cleaner sound by pedaling on each beat. At the height of the crescendo, prolong the pedal if you wish. Throughout this Nocturne, pedaling on each beat of those cascading 32nd notes will make for a more brilliant effect.

The *fortissimo* in bar 14 certainly would be helped by a pedal. The run that follows could be played without pedal, but after the *con forza* passage, it will sound rather pale. Try playing it with a pedal on each beat. The pedaling in bar 15 doesn't quite do the job. Try a pedal on the second, third, fourth and sixth beats.

As a general rule applicable in all the Nocturnes, pedal with each harmonic change. When the harmony does not change but you want a lighter, more delicate effect, change pedals. A good example of the latter occurs in bars 31-33. Instead of forcing the melody to compete with all those bass notes, pedal again on the fourth beat. In bar 33 each staccato note in the lowest voice should be pedaled.

Inexplicably, we locate a six-bar section, bars 34-39, without pedal marks. Everything that has been suggested thus far would be applicable here. Where you want a lighter, more delicate texture, as in bars 34-39, pedal more frequently. A special problem arises in bar 37. The low G cannot be sustained without pedal. But a sustained pedal muddies the sound, and it is preferable to pedal again on the fourth beat and let the G go. In bars 44-47 most of the chords are arpeggios and require pedal. But after they receive their full value, pedal again so that the upper voice can sound clean and uncluttered.

Another problem awaits in bars 50-53. The upper voice is to be played *pianissimo*, but the lower voices have the melody, *mezzo forte*, and must be sung out robustly, yet *legato* as well. The pedal will help with the latter, but it will also increase the resonance of the upper voice, which must float unobtrusively above. The single prolonged pedal in the Schirmer edition will not accomplish this, certainly not with the modern piano. Instead, produce the song with hand weight and *legato* action of the fingers, while using as little pedal as possible. Through experimentation you will come up with the best balance.

The passage beginning with bar 74 is another of those abrupt changes of mood that are so characteristic of Field's Nocturnes generally and this one in particular. But its relationship with the broader tone of the piece quickly becomes apparent with the return of the rising and falling 32nd notes. There is a tender moment on the third beat in bar 76, where a triplet is introduced at the end of the phrase. At this point, the assertive *forte* does not serve the music well. One possible alternative is a *diminuendo* beginning on the third beat of bar 75 and concluding with a *piano* in bar 76. Begin another crescendo on the sixth beat of bar 76, peaking on the fourth beat of bar 77. There is another *diminuendo* indicated in bar 79, but whatever preceded it is absent from this edition. A possible correction would be to play bar 78 *piano* or *pianissimo*, and begin another crescendo at the beginning of bar 79.

The prolonged pedal spanning bars 86-87 is ill advised when Field is asking for a *diminuendo*. Try lifting the pedal on the first beat of bar 87 and take that long run without pedal for a tonal texture that contrasts with the previous bar. If you prefer pedal on the first half of the run, then pedal with each beat. The hushed ending would benefit, as usual, by use of *una corda*.

Those readers who strive to project the introspective character of Nocturne Ten will encounter a variety of challenges and the necessity for numerous decisions. If you approach it as essentially idyllic, the task will be much less demanding. But by presenting this Nocturne to an audience as I have suggested, and by taking some chances, you might succeed in raising this music to the upper realms of romantic, lyrical expression.

CHAPTER FIFTEEN:

NOCTURNE NO. 11

This Nocturne was published in 1833, four years before Field's death. The historical record provides no clue regarding its date of composition. Field may have written it during the ten-year hiatus when he was overindulging in alcohol and in declining health, and decided to delay its publication.

During these final four years Field was also reworking Nocturne Number Ten; yet no two of his Nocturnes are greater contrasts of musical style than these. While Number Ten teemed with notes aloft and choirs of three or more voices, Number Eleven employs the sparest of means to tell its story.

Of the 118 bars, only thirty employ more than a simple upper and lower voice; and of those thirty, only one bar employs more than three voices. The opening five bars are so stark and repetitive, they foreshadow twentieth century minimalism. There is no audience-pleasing display of virtuosity here, no high drama. Pared down to the bare truth, this Nocturne impresses me as having been written for Field himself, a page in a musical diary. The story:

This is one of those quieter moments when I allow myself to be carried along by a mood that is not quite joy but rather a lull in the struggle. While I sing at my ease, I never cease to be aware of the transitory nature of all things, bright and dark. At times it is an effort to prevent the ache and the yearning from intruding and abruptly ending this lovely interlude. After all, we are soul mates and can never part. When I recall what we have been through and will continue to endure, I grow weary, so weary, contemplating the struggle. And sometimes I will rage against what is. Only the song can renew me, only the song will sustain me until the end.

Again Field returns to one of his favorite motifs, the repeated note that often seems to peal like a bell. The four B-flats that begin this Nocturne sound a bit solemn, certainly subdued. The B-flat is repeated sixteen more times as part of a sequence of triplets that gradually ascend by chromatic steps from D to B-flat an octave higher. Just before they reach that point, B-flat just below high C rings out three times, as though announcing that the introduction is over and now a stately procession begins.

This is a new approach for Field in the unfolding of his story, and there is about it something eerie. When the theme finally appears in the sixth bar, it begins on a lofty and rather lonely B-flat, more than an octave above the accompanying triplets. By some strange quirk of association, my mind leaps backwards to the poem by William Wordsworth that begins, "I wandered lonely as a cloud/that drifts o'er vales and hills." That haunting image suits the mood of this piece.

In these 118 bars, there are only seven accented notes, none of them *sforzando*, and four beats (octaves, not chords) played *forte*. Essentially, the story is told by that lone upper voice and the ever-present triplets below. If performed at the suggested MM of dotted quarter=100, this introspective wanderer would be scampering merrily through a Wordsworthian field of dandelions, much to the delight and approval of F. Liszt. I suggest setting your metronome at 69, or perhaps a notch higher. At a setting of 80 or 84, you will please the ear with a lovely song, but little more.

One's first impression may be that this is a relatively peaceful and charming idyllic interlude for Field. But the chromatic subtext, beginning in bar 2 and carried throughout this Nocturne in both clefs, is just one of several familiar motifs that identify this as an Introspective Nocturne. With the opening notes of the theme, we are met by one of Field's principal motifs, the yearning phrase. It is two bars long and marked *espressivo*, which immediately prepares us for an inward emotional journey and not a summer outing. The long yearning phrase is repeated in bars 10-11.

Despite the comforting and supportive triplets below, the motifs continue to tell their story. The accented notes in bar 12, motif #8, descend from G to F in what sounds like an extended sigh, motif #2, and should be delayed by a *sostenuto*. When we enter bar 13, the E-flat immediately leaps an octave, motif #10. But instead of the flight of 32nd notes that would have been launched in the earlier Nocturnes, the melodic line descends slowly in triplets, to begin another yearning phrase.

At this point, the story of this Nocturne appears to be one of resignation. The poet is free to sing and can take some pleasure in those notes above high C, but his aspirations have been tempered, the passion of his youth cooled. Within those parameters, we find the familiar mood, the play of contrasts, joy and melancholy, contentment and loss, and the moving forward. Not only the early chromatics but the harmonic shifting between major and minor that began in bar 4 instantly establish the introspective mood.

Taken at a quicker tempo, these harmonic nuances would be lost, particularly the more subtle ones. Example: in bar 5, the fourth triplet is B-flat with an augmented 5th and 6th arrived at chromatically from the preceding triplet and creating a minor second between the A and the high B-flat in the treble, motif #8, which hints at pain that will soon be more acute.

At the end of each of the early yearning phrases, the poet leaps ever higher, first to high C, then to E above high C, and then G, and finally A-flat, counterbalancing the melancholy with his song. The first admission of underlying pain occurs as a stabbing high A-flat in bar 29, after which the yearning phrases continue. Augmenting the stab is the trill on F-sharp in the same bar. This is a clash of two chords, an early example of bitonality, which Field learned from Beethoven. I suggest that this crescendo rise to a *mezzo forte*, followed by a *diminuendo* that is missing from this edition. Another crescendo, beginning in bar 35, also requires a peak and a *diminuendo*. Try a *mezzo forte* on the first beat of bar 37, and then come down. This scheme anticipates the *forte* in bar 39.

In bar 34 the fourth triplet, in B-flat, slips into a B-flat minor6 in bar 35. The 6th is the lowest note and the beginning of a brief duet that is continued by the low C in bar 36 and the thirds that follow in this and the next bar. This note also exerts a downward pull on the melody and foreshadows something darker to come. And it comes without delay in bar 36, where the triplets drop to their lowest point thus far. At the same time the first D-flat appears, high and prominent and forming a minor second with the C in the triplet. One of the lovelier harmonic sequences occurs in bars 35-38, making the mood richer and more complex.

The motifs that we have thus far encountered have been leading up to the first major change in mood, motif #5, beginning with the *forte* octave in bar 39. We have reached another level, signaled by the instruction to play this passage *espressivo*, which harks back to the first appearance of the theme in bar 6. This is surely a clear indication that Field wants the pianist to acknowledge and project the dark side of this Nocturne. This should be a bold, forthright *forte*, an emotional outburst that suggests a soliloquy, an argument with the self that continues in bars 43-45. We now have reason to question whether the theme of this story really is one of resignation and acceptance. Powerful and pervasive ambivalence is quintessential John Field.

The dynamic marks in bars 39-46 are perplexing and not at all helpful. In the middle of this dramatic passage the dynamics suddenly droop from *forte* to *piano*. Then follows a *diminuendo,* reducing the *piano* to an improbable and ineffective *pianissimo*. Where the *piano* is indicated, try substituting a *diminuendo,* ending on the first beat of bar 42, a C minor triad. Repeat this process in bars 43-45. These could be interpreted as prolonged yearning phrases, the leading motif in this piece.

In bar 46 we find what appears to be a superfluous instruction: *sempre legato il basso*. Well, of course. That's what we've been doing all along. This is Field's way of telling us to make more of the bass, to sing it so that we have a duet of nearly equal partners, motif #9. This duet contributes another emotional element that ends with an absent *diminuendo* in bar 50.

Field's inventiveness, the variety of ways in which he can project these emotions, is displayed in the long passage beginning with bar 59. Instead of a full bar played *forte*, he gives us an octave *forte,* followed by *piano*, a motif #3 outburst. Two more yearning phrases are followed by another *forte-piano*. He seems unable to contain himself. Resigned? Not quite. At peace with himself? Not quite. In bar 63, amid all this we hear a duet in sixths, followed by another lovely harmonic sequence of major and diminished chords. The crescendo that began in bar 64 should peak on the accented C, motif #8, in the next bar. A *diminuendo* to *piano* should follow but is not indicated. Neither the Peters nor the Kalmus editions corrects this omission.

In this same bar, Field returns to the repeated B-flat, which he last used in the duet passage, bars 46-50. He repeats the B-flat again one octave higher in bar 68. This motif, the repetition of the B-flat three or more times in succession, occurs seven times. The long-short-long rhythm that comes right out of Beethoven's Opus 27 No. 2 Adagio movement is an important component of the mood that Field creates in this Nocturne. One can only imagine the profound and lasting effect that the tolling of those repeated notes had on Field's imagination. Had he not written his ninth Nocturne, this allusion would be mere speculation.

Although it is not indicated with another *sempre legato il basso,* the duet reappears in bar 66 and ends with the *diminuendo* in bar 69. This duet introduces a passage of utterly transparent emotion. The mask is cast aside, and the underlying pathos is fully revealed The three high B-flats, tolling for the seventh and last time, introduce three sighs in the form of three descending triplets. In bar 70, the accented high B-flat is a stab that is followed by a *molto espressivo* and slowly descending sighs. But we have not yet touched bottom. Bar 73 is marked *pianissimo e languido.* This is not the languor of peace or respite. It is the expression of emotional exhaustion, and conveying this musically will be a challenging assignment. The entire passage, bars 71-74, should be played *a piacare,* with a gradual return to *a tempo* in bar 75. Notice also that as the melodic line descends in halting half steps, the first note of each phrase in the bass descends chromatically, from C-flat in bar 73 to G in bar 76. A slight emphasis on those notes is appropriate. In bar 76, ignore the *diminuendo,* which should begin in bar 77, as indicated.

There is no point of rest, of comfort, of untroubled bliss anywhere in this Nocturne. We may have been drawn in, at first, by the sweet innocence of the expansive melody; but with the return of the yearning phrases in bar 75, illusions are dispelled. When a flight occurs in bars 84-86, it is in 16ths and lacks the brilliance and élan of the soaring 32nd notes in several of the earlier Nocturnes, and its pinnacle is a single F above high C. Although the 16ths are set against a steady flow of triplets below, play them expressively, with some rhythmic freedom.

More than in any of the other Nocturnes, the harmonic underpinning of Number Eleven plays a major part in establishing the mood and telling the story. An excellent example of how Field artfully transcended the limits of conventional harmonic writing can be found in the passage beginning at bar 82 and ending at 94. The passage begins in E-flat, the tonic. The triplets below will be forming the chord progressions; but for the next nine bars the third note of each triplet will strike E-flat, regardless of the chord. Wherever the harmony may wander, that E-flat stands unmoved, a kind of pedal point. This arrangement supports the melody nicely when the chord is E-flat or A-flat. In B-flat, however, the low E-flat becomes an abrasive diminished fifth, repeated four times in bar 85. Another device for stirring emotion and deviating from the expected is to comfortably establish the tonic for three beats and, on the fourth beat augment the fifth of the chord, as in bars 82 and 86. A variation of this occurs in bar 89 where the triplets in A-flat play against the 16th notes that waver between B and C, forming alternately major and minor harmonies.

This undercurrent of restlessness, tension and non-fulfillment takes a new direction in bar 90. Suddenly *pianissimo,* the music drifts away from the key center. From E-flat it slips into E by way of a B7 chord. Now, instead of repeating an E-flat four times to the bar, we have a repeated B. This soul is a wanderer without an emotional center. The fateful repeated notes also reappear in the upper voice with G-sharp tolling three times in bar 91, and A four times in bar 93. On the fourth stroke it is the 7th of a B7 chord with a diminished 5th that brings us back to the dominant B-flat of the original key.

As one has come to expect, with the return of the home key the yearning phrases reappear, three in succession. Where will this end? How much more story does this Nocturne have to tell? We need not wait long for an answer. In bar 102 the song diminishes to a mysterious triple *piano*, a dynamic that rarely occurs in these Nocturnes before the ultimate bar. To achieve the maximum effect, use of *una corda* is essential. After a two-beat pause, the melody leaps to E-flat ten steps above high C, a height attained only once before, in the freewheeling Nocturne Ten. This is an extraordinary moment and unique in these eighteen Nocturnes. It is as though the spirit has suddenly been released from the body and all its attendant cares. For seven bars this ethereal state continues without deviation from the triple *pianissimo*. There is not an accented note, not a single tiny crescendo.

The very instant the high E-flat is lightly struck, the melodic line begins its descent haltingly, a triplet followed by an octave drop, three successive times. The triplets below are still grounded, repeating B-flat on the third note of each triplet while restlessly changing the harmony on each beat. The melody, a model of simplicity, floats along purely in the E-flat diatonic scale, while the bass is churning out major, minor, diminished, and abrasive chords with diminished 5ths. This is another expression of the ambivalence in Field's music, the pull in opposite directions.

When the melodic line reaches its lowest point, the E-flat then steps above middle C and a series of two-note phrases in 16ths begins. They could be interpreted as a succession of sighs, or the hyperventilating of someone who is unable to speak. This is all happening in the preternatural hush of the triple *piano*, still without an accent or a minor crescendo. After eight repetitions there is an abrupt change in the mood. This muted gasping must now accelerate to *allegretto* and crescendo to a peak of hysteria ten triplets later. While the lower voice obstinately repeats a B-flat7 triad four times in each bar, the gasping phrases rise chromatically, a half step with each triplet. Major and minor 2nds crackle with almost every beat. The atmosphere is electric with untranslatable anguish until the *diminuendo* and *rallentando* in bar 112 return us to the sanity of Tempo I and a melodic line that calmly proceeds scale-wise, apparently no worse for the experience.

The concluding four bars are not the standard-issue *rallentando* and *diminuendo* but rather a brief passage that perfectly concludes this drama. Starting at the E-flat that marked the return to Tempo I, we proceed stepwise upward with a sort of limp, a sequence of quarter notes followed by eighth notes, until we reach that very high, magical mystical E-flat, triple *piano*. This limping figure was first introduced in bar 73, marked *languido,* when the poet seemed to have reached his lowest point. If Field wanted to portray a wounded bird-like spirit determined to continue singing its song, he could not have done much more with his material than he has done here. This is pathos portrayed in as nearly pure a form as I can imagine. At the end, he does not ask for a mere *rallentando.* He wants *perdendo* and *sostenuto,* a lingering demise.

Some readers may feel that this analysis lost its way in the Land of Melodrama, and that the author is looking for and, alas, finding emotion and meaning that is not there. It is possible—and probable, if Liszt were conducting this tour—that another interpreter could see bar 102 as an apotheosis in which the mysterious poet achieves his ultimate desire. Consequently, he would see the hyperventilating in bars 107-112 as unfettered exuberance and joy. In his chapter on Field's Nocturnes, Piggott refers to the sudden change in mood at bar 49 as ". . . an impassioned outburst in C minor: it is as if a sudden storm cloud had thrown its shadow over a moonlit landscape. This brief darkening of mood occurs twice . . . but these elements in no way disturb the rapt calm of the music . . ." I see yearning, anguish and pathos; Mr. Piggott sees rapt calm. Differences such as these make art of any kind an endlessly fascinating subject.

Mr. Piggott also describes this Nocturne as a ". . . neglected masterpiece . . . one of the peaks of his achievement." We could not be in more complete agreement. My double regret is that it may never be heard for the masterpiece that it actually is. John O'Conor's recorded performance of Number Eleven presents us with an enchanting, lovely Idyll, and no more.

Before departing, the matter of pedaling must be addressed. Since for some reason no pedaling at all is given, we start with a blank slate. As always, your interpretation of the music should determine the use of pedal. For example, for the first five bars you may try omitting pedal, or applying pedal on each beat, keeping it as clean and stark as possible. However, if you see this as Mr. Piggott does, an evening idyll, you will probably want to soften the texture and use pedal from the start.

Either way, bar 6 should be pedaled by changing with each note in the melody, or twice per bar. As always, where the harmony changes, pedaling is desirable. In the earlier passage, try to convey a feeling of innocence that is periodically ruffled and disturbed. This is a superb melody, the equal of any fashioned by Schubert. Both the Peters and Kalmus editions do a good job of providing pedal marks that will assist in bringing out the melody. But I cannot recommend either edition for its guidance in dynamics.

In bar 46, where the duet begins, the lower voice, despite the wide intervals, must be *legato*; so, unless you have extraordinarily large hands, apply the pedal with each beat. Beginning with bar 113, pedal each triplet in order to produce a fluid and unaccented *legato* in the lower voice. And finally, try dying away *una corda*.

CHAPTER SIXTEEN:

NOCTURNE NO. 12

Titled "Nocturne Caracteristic—Noontide" in the Schirmer edition, simply "Midi" in Peters, where it is number Eighteen, and "Nocturne Caracteristic—Midi" in Kalmus, it is not a Nocturne at all, by even the broadest possible interpretation of the genre. This is what Mr. Piggott informs us:

This work first appeared in 1810 as the Premier Divertissement, with a string quartet accompaniment. It was reprinted under various titles, but never as a nocturne. In 1832 it was published in France as "Midi—Nocturne Caracteristique," along with the publisher's false claim that it was written in Paris. Despite its falling outside the genre, Liszt included it in his 1869 edition of Field's Nocturnes. Piggott concludes: "Future editions of Field's Nocturnes should exclude it."

Once again, Mr. Piggott and I are in harmonious agreement. But it is a lovely piece of music, John Field at his most playful and charming. It is filled with delightful, chromatic harmonies, changes of mood and key, and syncopated rhythm.

The Allegro called for at the head of the music is absurd. An allegretto at MM quarter note=104 would serve the music much better. Since no pedaling is indicated, this piece would be a good exercise in experimenting with pedal, including when to omit it in certain passages. I hope that teachers of piano performance who read this will consider assigning it to intermediate students and including it in recitals. Midi deserves to be heard.

But number Twelve is not a Nocturne.

CHAPTER SEVENTEEN:

NOCTURNE NO. 13

This Nocturne (Number Seven in the Peters edition) could not have been written by a young John Field. Number Thirteen tells a story with significant differences from the others. Here we find a more mature, philosophical poet who recognizes certain truths about himself, reality, and his role in the world. But this knowledge does not entirely free him from the yearning and struggle that have been his lot. As a poet he cannot stop dreaming or striving against limitation and circumstance. When his dream appears to be fading, he responds with greater determination to continue singing, because the song is all that he has.

This is the poet's story:

Tonight my dream is not about achievement, acclaim, or self-expression. It is about a deeper need that I have never acknowledged before. My dream is of love, a true and lasting soul-nourishing love. It is not as brilliant or dramatic as my song, though more profound, and more enduring. In my dream I can imagine my love, and the image lifts me up until I feel transcendent. Then there are moments when I ache with the longing, and rail against the possibility—even the probability—that the dream will remain a mere phantom, a vain aspiration. I despair and sing my heart out to relieve the pain and share it with the world. Thus many a lonely evening ends with yearning and sighs as I revisit the dream that will not release me.

I came to understand that the Sognante posted at the start should not be interpreted as referring to a dream, but rather a dream-like state of reverie and contemplation. The poet in this story is awake and aware. The appearance of the melody in the inner voice, rather than aloft, is the poet's acknowledgement of the human condition and his own place in the world. His nature and his needs will never change. This is expressed in the melody that hovers around middle C and, with few exceptions, moves stepwise. Except for some variation in sonority, it repeats itself exactly, numerous times.

The G just below high C becomes symbolic of the poet's limits, within which he tries to find solace and contentment. The accents on many of the G's also reveal his resistance to those limits. Once again, this is the ambivalent John Field. He is goaded by that stabbing G, which also serves as the apex of a series of leaps and yearning phrases. The motif #1 shifts to the bass clef in bars 13-14, where a crescendo applies only to the lower voices, indicating that this yearning is an intrinsic part of the poet's nature and speaks from a profound need. In the opening section there are also sighs, bars 18 and 26. This is, indeed, an Introspective Nocturne.

The *smorzando* in bar 33 represents a weariness, possibly a flagging of faith. The poet's response is a renewed determination and greater effort, expressed in the *agitato* at bar 35. The melody is repeated a half step higher, and the top note is now A, a step higher than G, and gradually even higher, peaking at G above high C.

After this response, the poet returns to his familiar song, which is unchanged by the experience. Shortly he is rewarded for his persistence and devotion to the dream: in bars 51-53 he feels as though his spirit has been released, and for a moment he is free of his bonds and his striving. With not the slightest effort, he floats up to C above high C.

When he returns to earth in bar 54, his song is repeated a step higher, as it appeared during the *agitato* passage, bars 35-38. Now, however, he sings with greater assurance and composure for ten bars. As we have come to expect, he is never free of his ambivalence for long. The cycle returns and he is hyperanxious again, determined to assert himself and keep the dream alive. Rushing ahead, *forte,* he strikes that G above high C three times, on the first beat of bars 64-66.

Having made his mark, the poet returns to his original song, exactly as he first sang it. And again he experiences release, rising up to that magical-mystical C above high C. Ah, that is the true reward for not abandoning the dream and the song.

If we expect at this point that the poet has told his story and has nothing left to reveal, we are mistaken. As he strikes the G below high C three times in bar 77, the lower voices are softly sighing in unison. Despite the poet's efforts, his soaring up above high C, proving that all is well, the sighing resumes *pianissimo* in bar 81, and again triple *piano* in bar 83. There will be a final nearly inaudible chord, and the story will end rather sadly.

No! This poet is not leaving so quietly on such a melancholy note. He returns to his song, the version that is one half step higher, a significant and vital step. Shortly he leaps again to G above high C, and once again—determined that this time the story will not end with those pathetic sighs of defeat—he climbs, he soars with ease to C above high C.

This is a story of considerable passion and struggle; but it is also grounded and well balanced. Now we face the question of how best to perform this emotionally complex and technically challenging Nocturne.

The voice of the poet is in the top note of each chord. This presents some problems, both technical and interpretive. The top note must be clearly distinguished from the others. This is best accomplished by applying more hand weight to that note and less to the others, and doing it consistently if you are to avoid disrupting the melodic line. You must sing out the melody expressively, and with rhythmic flexibility, so we are not just hearing a sequence of plodding chords. Although not indicated in the score, the 32nd note turns should be softer than the lower voices. Only the accented bell-like G should stand out.

None of the above can be accomplished if taken at an inappropriate tempo. The MM following the Sognante is much too fast and is contraindicated both technically and interpretively. I evoke this dream with MM quarter note=56. Experimentation will determine, as always, what is right for each pianist.

One run-through of this Nocturne will demonstrate that many of the chords cannot be struck at once and require the *arpeggio*. In the Schirmer's edition, an *arpeggio* is indicated only once, on the first beat of bar 6. No *simile* suggests that the *arpeggio* should be used with similar chords; but necessity dictates that it must. In the Peters edition, *arpeggios* in the bass abound and are indicated even when not required. The purpose, evidently, is to create a harp-like Irish-bard accompaniment in a heavily edited version of this Nocturne that perverts Field's intentions.

While the dream-like state will soon enough be disturbed, a contrasting calm must first be established. Thus, the lower voices must sound effortless, rather than edgy and breathless. Achieving this is another reason for a slower tempo. The first chord in bar 6 is particularly awkward and requires unconventional fingering. I play it as an *arpeggio* up to the B, and then cross the second finger over the thumb to land the melody note.

In bar 10, a pause before the 32nd notes—which are a written-out turn introducing the accented G—would be interpretively justified. This also applies to bar 54.

The passage beginning *piu agitato* at bar 35 and extending to bar 46 is the second subject of this Nocturne. No accented notes or *sforzanados* appear in any of these bars, so the agitation must come from a hastening of the tempo, rhythmic flexibility, and dynamic contrasts. Instead of performing bars 35-43 *mezzo forte,* as indicated in the score, try a sequence of crescendos and *diminuendos,* from *piano* to *mezzo forte.*

I hasten the tempo just a bit because the *stringendo* that appears in bar 44 requires an even faster tempo. I also build a crescendo up to *forte* on the first beat of bar 38, diminish to *piano* in bar 39, start another crescendo in bar 40, build to a *mezzo forte* on the first beat of bar 42, and diminish to *piano* in bar 43. After the *diminuendo* in bar 45, *ritardando* is absolutely necessary, followed by *a tempo* in bar 47.

The most prominent motif in this section is #8, which occurs in almost every bar. There are two abrasive minor seconds in bar 35, three in bar 36, and three more in bar 37. At the end of bar 44 there is a lacerating chord that probably defies analysis. This is more than adventurous harmonic writing. It is defiance, approximating in sound what Field was experiencing.

At bar 51 the score calls for a crescendo, but I am unable to comply. This brief but exquisite passage of spiritual release is best expressed *pianissimo.* The Peters and Kalmus editions disagree, instructing that it be played *mezzo forte* or *forte.* They both solve the problem of the first *piu agitato* by eliminating it! With regard to dynamics, those editions are no help.

From bar 75 onward to the end, we continue to encounter the introspective motifs with even greater frequency, and in new combinations. Following motif #1 in bars 75-76, we find motif #2, three sighs with that haunting G repeated a sixth above. When a fourth is added to the G chord in bars 77, 81 and 83, we hear a pang with those sighs. The poet finds some relief for one bar with the C and C7, but the G4 is repeated. If performed with sensitivity, the pathos of this passage becomes unmistakably exposed.

In the concluding sixteen bars, the dominant of the key, G, continues to prevail, a stroke in each bar, but not with the clarity and peal of the early passage. In bar 92, eight bars before the end, the magical G above high C is struck lightly, gently, and once again in the next bar. Then the theme begins a slow descent, and we sense that the poet is returning to earth to face the inevitable truth. Field closes the story with a final phrase that begins on the G above high C and ends on a higher C, the highest note attained in this Nocturne, now *estinto,* dying away. As he does so, he includes two faintly perceptible sighs. The upper note is the E on the third beat of bar 96, and the lower note is the middle C on the first beat of bar 97. This figure is repeated in bars 97-98. Give those notes just a little extra sonority.

Several technical matters need attention. The *forte* in bar 19 supposedly must be maintained until the *diminuendo* in bar 26. This is contrary to the character of this piece. Try diminishing on the third beat of bar 21, with a *piano* by the third beat of the next bar. A second crescendo could begin immediately and peak on the first beat of bar 24, *mezzo forte*. A third crescendo could peak on the first beat of bar 26, followed by the *diminuendo* that is already indicated.

The *smorzando* in bar 33 is really a request to diminish and retard a little, with a return to tempo on the third beat of bar 34.

In the passage beginning at bar 55, we have another instance of a dynamic extending inappropriately for nine bars. One solution, dictated by what precedes and follows this passage, is a *diminuendo* in bar 58 to *piano* or *pianissimo* in bar 59, and another crescendo to *mezzo forte* on the first beat of bar 62. Then diminish to *piano* in bar 63, where the *stringendo* episode returns. A *rallentando* should accompany the *diminuendo* in bar 65, with an *a tempo* in bar 67.

If you follow the crescendo in bar 71, begin *pianissimo* and go no louder than a *mezzo piano*. Those high notes would not be happy with a *mezzo forte* and, I suspect, neither would John Field.

Dynamic marks are also missing in bar 80. The crescendo starting in bar 78 must peak somewhere. Place it on the first beat of bar 80, *mezzo piano,* and then diminish to the *pianissimo*. The *mezzo forte* in bar 85 also requires a *diminuendo*. Placing it at the third beat of bar 87 will work well.

I like to post a Poco Meno Mosso at bar 94 and start a *rallentando* on the third beat of bar 96. This ending strikes me as more supportive of the story, the poet's resistance to seeing the dream end.

Regarding use of the pedal, I suggest a fresh pedal with each note of the melody in bars 3-10. When the 32nd notes are added, starting at bar 11, pedal on the first and third beats. Where the upper voice is unaccompanied, try omitting the pedal. In bars 22 and 26 a pedal on each beat would clarify the phrasing. In bar 77, pedal on each beat. *Una corda* in bar 83 will help to reduce the resonance of the bass. In the last eight bars, use of pedal on each beat will produce a more delicate effect. The final three bars would also benefit by applying *una corda*.

Nocturnes Ten and Thirteen are technically among the most difficult, especially so for non-professionals and students. I urge you not to be discouraged if you are not making beautiful music after two or three hours of diligent practice. Eventually you will be rewarded. There is a great deal of beauty and emotion here to be experienced and shared.

CHAPTER EIGHTEEN:
NOCTURNE NO. 14

This Nocturne is another that could not have been written by the young John Field. In common with Number Thirteen, its true character, the story, evolved for me over a considerable period. The introspective motifs dominated, and I could hear only the yearning and sighing of an aspiring poet. But now I am totally convinced that no one of these Nocturnes can be comprehended without the perspective that comes of knowing them all. As my understanding deepened, I began to see Number Fourteen as a love song.

The introspective motifs did not vanish. They became absorbed into a love song that encompasses the full range of emotion, from ardor to tenderness, and includes the ache and the longing and the nuances of deep emotion. In twenty-four miraculous bars, the story of love finds expression.

The languid simplicity of the melody is set against a constantly moving harp-like figure in the bass that rises gracefully and returns. The tempo indicator at the head is Lento. This is followed, in the perverse fashion that so distinguishes this edition, with MM 8th=108. Played at this speed, a gem of lyrical romantic expression becomes merely an etude for the promotion of dexterity in the left hand, and a vehicle for impressing an audience with your flashy technique. The Peters and Kalmus editions remedy this error by posting a MM 8th=80. At this tempo you will hear a pretty tune, but not much more. Try performing this one at 8th=69, a tempo that allows all the harmonic modulations, chromatics, nuances and phrasing to breathe.

This is another of the later Nocturnes that stand midway between the Introspective and the Idyllic. Several subtle variants of the ten motifs are here, almost all of which would be lost to the ear at a too-quick tempo. Among the unforgivable losses are brief, chromatic phrases that are so delicate, yet so intensely moving, they can break your heart if they catch you during a weak moment.

The lower voice should be played as *legato* as possible, without accents, and kept under the melody. The accompaniment keeps one so busy, there may be a tendency to forget that the melodic upper voice must never stop singing in a *bel canto* style. The insistent regularity of the lower voice may also lead to an overly regular pulse, but this should be avoided. This love song requires, demands, thrives on expressive flexibility.

One of the places where your musical intuition comes into play is bar 6, beats three, four and five. These 32nd note triplets would adore a *sostenuto* as they swell and climb. The first three beats of the next bar should also be played expressively.

In bar 8, the first motif #1 begins with the three 8th notes. The poignant expression of yearning suggests that this could be a story of unrequited love. There should be a crescendo that peaks *mezzo forte* on the first beat of bar 9, followed by a *diminuendo*. The second yearning phrase, a much more elaborate one, begins on the third beat of bar 9. The crescendo is already indicated, but there is no *diminuendo*, which should begin on the third beat of bar ten and end *piano* in bar 11. Here the harmony changes with each beat, from D to A-sharp diminished, to B minor, to E minor, to D and C-sharp minor, giving us our first motif #6. This is also one of the places where the harp-like figure is replaced by a simple broken chord, which becomes a duet. I suspect that Field may have done this to bring out the harmonic sequence. If your sense of this music leads you to agree, you will then want to make the bass a little more prominent here. This also occurs in bars 8, 12, 13, 19, 20 and 21.

In bar 13 we have an affecting combination of motifs: motif #6 in the harmonic movement from A minor to C dim., to G, to A minor, and finally to a clash of major and minor modes on the sixth beat, which is our motif #8. The shifting of the lower voice between the diatonic and the chromatic creates passing major and minor seconds, which contributes to the pleasure, pain and urgency of the emotion, especially if it pertains to unrequited love.

The only instance in which the lower voice has a singing role occurs in the next bar. For nine beats the roles are switched and we have a true duet. It starts out simply, in the tonic and dominant, but there is little delay in sending the upper voice on a chromatic flight while the lower voice continues its statement. That lower line moves steadily upward in a crescendo from G to E just above middle C at the end of the phrase. However, the melodic line actually ends on the A in the treble with an octave, *forte*.

This brief shift of attention away from the principal singer suggests that the poet is speaking in his own voice, from the depths of his being. This is more than a song, he may be telling us. This is a passionate confession. The only *forte* in these twenty-four bars occurs at the end of this statement, indicating its importance as the emotional center of the Nocturne.

Further comment on the confession comes out in bar 16. On the third beat, the dynamic level suddenly drops without a *diminuendo* from *forte* to *piano,* and we are given the instruction to perform this passage *teneramente*. This is a masterful and utterly affecting contrast to the preceding passage. A captive of his emotions, the poet is pulled from one expression of his love to another.

In the Schirmer edition, the *teneramente* is placed between two lines and thus might be taken to apply to bar 14. But the Peters and Kalmus editions eliminate possible confusion by placing it between the staves in bar 16. In its response to the preceding utterance in the bass, this bar gives us a sigh that begins on the sixth beat and concludes on the first beat of bar 17. The last three beats of that bar prepare us for another sigh and should be played expressively. We are very much in the realm of the Introspective Nocturne at this point.

In bar 17 a crescendo is called for, beginning with the first beat and peaking at the accented high C. Otherwise, dynamically this passage makes no sense. Neither the Kalmus nor the Peters edition makes this correction. After the high C, begin the *diminuendo.*

Following this tender and emotion-filled moment, the song returns, in bar 18, to the steady calm of the dominant and tonic of the key. But in this short Nocturne, Field cannot linger there. Within two phrases, both ending with a sigh, he takes us for an emotional ride from G to E7, to A minor, to G, to C7, to D11, to D and back to G. Part of the effectiveness of this passage is the subdued downward movement, in contrast to the swelling ascent of the song in bar 15. Again, this is the ambivalent Field, the poet being tossed about in the sea of emotion, sometimes on the crest of a wave, sometimes in its trough. Just when we are led to believe that the pangs of longing are over, on the fourth beat of bar 17, a voice from the treble drops to its lowest point, an A below middle C. This is part of a D11 chord, with its prominent 2nd at the top.

We are not yet allowed to ease into the comfort of the tonic G. This is an ongoing story of love's pleasure and pain and unresolved emotions. In bar 20 there are three beats in G, followed by a delicate bitonal phrase, E minor in the bass, a tender flow of notes in the treble, the beats alternately chromatic and diatonic. This stripping away of everything but the essential emotion is something that Field and the best of the romantics do so well.

In bar 21 we continue in the minor mode, A minor, back to G, and then a pause. Field's sense of drama does not desert him here. What next? A quiet ending? A surprise? Field chooses a simple and touching conclusion. The subdominant, the tonic, and we return to the bitonality of bar 20, this time *dolcissimo*. This is your invitation to caress this music and savor even the minor seconds.

Nocturne Fourteen has the conciseness, depth of feeling and elevated language of a fine poem. An effective performance requires that the pianist get inside the story and become the lovesick poet.

As usual, the pedal marks are inadequate. The Peters edition does a very good job of correcting these deficiencies, and the Kalmus edition is adequate. Peters adds a pedal on the last three beats of bars 8 and 10. In bar 11, which is devoid of pedal in Schirmer, Peters asks for pedal on each beat. Also add pedal on the third and fourth beats of bar 12. In all similar passages, add the missing pedal.

There are bars in which Schirmer prolongs the pedal inappropriately. In bar 20 the descending 32nd notes would be more delicate if the pedal were changed on each beat. I also add pedal on the second and third beats of bar 21. The same suggestion applies to the long run marked *dolcissimo*. However, if the pianist wishes to build the sonority at the beginning, follow the indicated pedaling. On the descent back to *pianissimo*, the effect will be enhanced by a pedal on each of the last three beats in bar 23. A *sostenuto* going into the last bar would be appropriate, with a slight *ritardando* at the end.

Before departing, I would like to offer another example of the wide divergence of opinion on Field and his music. Mr. Piggott, in his chapter on the Nocturnes says: "The principal interest of this piece, apart from its charming melody, lies in the harp-like accompaniment . . . It is not necessary to linger over this work . . . Its melancholy does not go very deep . . . It is music of an agreeable, domestic charm, but with little of the romantic lyricism we associate with Field's works in the nocturne genre."

It is possible that Mr. Piggott never heard a good performance of this Nocturne. I expect the reader to come to his or her own conclusions, but not before allowing the music to make it way into your bloodstream and the uncharted territory of spirit.

CHAPTER NINETEEN:

NOCTURNE NO. 15

This Nocturne is not numbered in the Schirmer edition. It simply has the sub-title, "Song Without Words." It is Number Thirteen in the Peters edition. On a first or even a second and third hearing, the pianist is apt to be disappointed, because this one bears so little resemblance to the others. Perhaps it really is simply a song.

I will now end the suspense. Unlike Number Twelve, this is a Nocturne, and before the close of this chapter I will confirm the presence of all ten motifs.

After playing Number Fifteen the first time, I was impressed by its utter simplicity. It has none of the embellishments and brilliant passages of the earlier Nocturnes. Instead, Field packed into this relatively short piece the intensity of expression that we expect in the slow movements of Beethoven's piano sonatas. Some time later, while doing research for this book, I came across the Largo that provided Field with the elements that he absorbed, by a kind of osmosis, and transformed into this Nocturne. But first, the poet's story:

At times, in moments of solitude, I fall into a mood of sadness that holds me in thrall. All of my efforts fail to break its grip. But I persist and, yes, I remember kind words, a smile, a pleasant hour with friends, and my spirit brightens as the burden lifts. Happiness is possible, I cry out, asserting myself against the gloom that would smother me. But the night is moonless and starless, the solitude unbroken, and my cry becomes one of anguish and desperation. Sadness is my companion, and my song is still.

Field may have intended this piece as a song, but of course it was Liszt who included it in the collected Nocturnes long after Field's death. Liszt probably was not impressed with it, but if he could include a rondo, why not this odd bird? Cast in a minor key, it is as spare as an elegy. Its tonal range is narrower than any of the others, rising only once to an A below high C. The aura of melancholy is largely derived from a melodic line that usually hovers around middle C, and a bottom-heavy bass that drops to C two octaves below middle C seven times in 69 bars.

The principal character of the theme is a downward drift, one slowly descending phrase followed by another, and yet another. In the first 32 bars there are only two 16th notes. In the middle section, the change of key to D major and five bars with 16th and 32nd notes allow more light to come through and briefly give wing to the spirit.

Despite its restricted range, this Nocturne is harmonically rather adventurous. There are bars in which the chord changes on every beat, and others in which they change on every 8th note, six changes per bar. Only a well-trained ear could follow all of the progressions, but these shifting harmonies create the inner glow of the music.

The ever-present undercurrent of emotion can be found in the many details that tell this story. The first occurs in bar 1, the leap of twelve steps from D to F, motif #10. There is a variant of motif #1 in bars 4 and 5. Instead of rising, there is a crescendo of three E's at the apex. A more emphatic motif #1 occurs in bars 8 and 9, where an E one octave higher is repeated five times, four of them as part of a triad.

In the first four bars, we find not only several chromatics that provide an edginess to the mood, motif #8, but an aura of longing in the shift from minor to diminished to major and back to minor. There is a lovely modulation in bar 6 that leads to the key of F major, a forecasting of the middle section, which is in a major key. In several bars, the sad downward movement of the phrase is accompanied by a sequence of chord changes. In bar 10, for example, we have: D minor7, B-flat minor9, A minor, G minor, F and C7.

If the listener has any doubt, up to this point, that this is going to be an intense emotional experience, that notion is dispelled in bars 12-14. The phrase begins *espressivo* and is followed by four heavily accented notes in both clefs. With the direction to play this passage expressively, there is no doubt that the accented notes must be dwelt on, *sostenuto*. This is a brief duet between upper and lower voices in sighs of longing, a figure so important to the story, it is repeated in bars 20-23.

This thirty-two bar section ends with two long yearning phrases that rise in a little crescendo with repeated notes, as they did in bars 8 and 9. But here the repetition is a third lower. The second of the two motifs #1 peaks with a *sforzando*, emphasizing the depth and urgency of the emotion. Coming just before the change to D major, this *sforzando* keeps in perspective and tempers any solace that the poet may take in the middle section.

The change of key begins with a Piu Moto, which should be just a notch or two above Tempo I. The Schirmer edition calls for a starting tempo of MM quarter note=80, which is consistent with the inappropriate tempi suggested throughout this volume. Much more suitable to the story would be quarter note=60. Any setting slower than that would tend to create a mood too somber and elegiac. The Piu Moto would then be set at 63, and no higher than 66.

Marked *dolce*, the theme remains essentially the same downward movement of 8th notes. Do the accents in bars 33 and 34 augment the sweetness? I think not. This is the ambivalent Field again. Despite the brighter key and livelier tempo, the yearning does not abate. The last two notes of the phrase, the accented E and D, are very much a sigh. And the *arpeggio* chords in the bass are a feeble attempt at joy.

Once again, the score calls for a *piu agitato* when no specific call for agitation appeared previously. Unlike Nocturne Thirteen, where this directive may suggest a reinterpretation of the entire piece, the *piu agitato* here refers to the Piu Moto in bar 32. It is still a vague and confusing mark. *Poco agitato*, or simply *agitato* would have been more understandable. There should also be an *a tempo* posted in bar 40 after the staccato notes. A second *agitato* would be effective in bar 52, coinciding with the *forte*. *A tempo* should then follow in bar 56.

In bar 43 we find the only motif #4; but this one is so restrained, it actually adds to the pathos. Rather than flying up to the *fermata*, this calls for a *sostenuto*.

Immediately after this aborted flight of 32nd notes, we have our first motif #3, the sudden outburst of four *sforzandos*, two of which are doubled in the treble. Here motif #3 is blended with #2 as these short phrases form a sequence of three sighs. This is transcendent agitation and the end of the sweetness. The sighs merge into a duet, motif #9, when the upper and lower voices complement each other.

The drama continues with two bars of relative calm, a return to the five descending notes that have become the principal motif of this Nocturne. Two bars are all we are allowed before the heavily accented notes return, followed by an even sharper accent in bar 50, accompanied by a stab of pain in the bass clef, motif #8. Again we have two bars of calm, suggesting that peace and joy may prevail. Perhaps, but not before a fierce struggle. The only motif #7 begins in bar 52 and continues through bar 53. Without a warning crescendo, suddenly *forte*, the poet reaches down to a G-sharp below middle C and begins a lurching upward two-octave climb to G. At the apex of his climb, two sharply accented thirds ring out. These are not bells but clarions, harsh and defiant. In the next bar they ring out again.

This passage always reminds me of those oft-quoted lines from a Dylan Thomas poem: "Do not go gentle into that good night/but rage, rage against the dying of the light." No words of mine could express it as well.

After this, the Nocturne slowly, inexorably returns to a series of small, yearning phrases and sighs. The abrupt return of Tempo I and the minor key without a *ritardando* or *rallentando* emphasizes the contrast between the two sections and increases the pathos, as though that were really necessary. If your heart is not already aching, Field will insure that it does, in bars 60-61. In a farewell gesture, the theme takes another leap of an octave, to high D, accented and part of a G major chord. This is delayed for just a moment with a *rallentando* before drooping to G minor.

The last eight bars could have been a quiet fading away, a formality. But the two yearning phrases cry out *sforzanado* at their apex. There really is no resolution. The pain, the longing will go on. This is affirmed in bars 67-68, where an A11 chord is held suspended for five long beats. Finally the C-sharp dissolves into the tonic D, and the eleventh doubles the tonic in the bass.

One must be moved and impressed by how Field does so much with such meager means. This is an intensely personal poem written in the simplest language, a language that was taught to him by Beethoven. I have not a shred of doubt that Field was an avid and careful student of Beethoven's piano sonatas, those German dish rags. If you have the score of his Opus 10 No. 3, turn to the second movement, Largo e Mesto (melancholy). Number Fifteen is not the obvious parody of the Opus 27 No. 2 that we found in the ninth Nocturne; but even a cursory examination of this Largo will reveal a stunning number of parallels that are difficult to dismiss.

Both are in triple meter, Beethoven in 6/9, Field in ¾. Both begin in the key of D minor. Both are in a slow tempo, Largo and Lento. Both have a principal theme that moves in 8th notes and hovers around middle C. Both have a predominance of phrases that descend, rather than rise. Both include an early leap of an octave. Both include repeated notes as a prominent motif. Both frequently erupt with *sforzandos* in a *piano* or *pianissimo* passage. Both alternate the *sforzandos* between the clefs. Both alternate reposeful passages with explosive ones. Both bristle with chromatics and passing notes that form major and minor seconds. Somewhere around the middle of each piece, the mode changes from minor to major. Field goes from D minor to D major,

Beethoven from D minor to B-flat major, although he does not change the key signature. The Largo ends with a long coda, unlike the Nocturne. But Field makes use of the coda in his Nocturne Number Three, where he places the melodic line in the treble, the accompaniment in the bass. At the concluding three measures of each composition, both use a suspended chord with a minor second before resolving into the tonic. And finally, both use all ten of the introspective motifs.

If you are following in the Peters or Kalmus editions, you probably have noticed that the MM directions are more sensible than the Schirmer's, but still too fast. Both editions do a pretty decent job of providing pedal marks. Both edit out all of the accents, except the *sforzandos* in the middle section, and eliminate the *piu agitato*. All this tampering is consistent with the attempts of both editions to sweeten and mellow Field a la the Liszt-Irish school.

In common with several other Nocturnes, including numbers 11, 12 and 13, there is either a dearth of pedal marks or a total absence in the Schirmer edition. Use of pedal in this Nocturne is extremely important and requires close attention, both to the score and to the effect that is being produced. This is particularly critical in bars with rapid changes of harmony, chromatics, and passing tones. In general, in order to avoid blurring the harmony, the legato effect should be achieved just with the fingers whenever possible. Pedal may be used to increase the sonority of a crescendo or an accented note.

Some examples, applicable throughout: in bar 3, pedal the third beat, and the first beat in bar 4. The same applies in bars 8 and 9. The second and third beats of bar 9, as well as in similar figures, should be played without pedal. In bars 13 and 14, pedal on the accented beats to increase sonority. Without question, the first beat of bars 29 and 31 require pedal, but the second and third do not.

In his chapter on the Nocturnes, Mr. Piggott devotes half a sentence—that is not a misprint—half a sentence to the fifteenth, known as "Song Without Words." It appears in the Peters edition as Number Thirteen and he lumps it together with Number Twelve: "It is not necessary to linger over this work, or over the Thirteenth Nocturne, in D minor . . ." The reader is left to assume that his basis for dismissing the Twelfth applies equally to the Thirteenth. The remainder of the quote appears at the conclusion of Chapter Eighteen.

There are at least two factors working here that shaped Mr. Piggott's verdict. One is that he has too narrow an understanding of the Nocturne which, as Field so skillfully demonstrates, may fall under a wide spectrum of expression, style and form. The second is that the language of this Nocturne is so simple, so direct and unadorned, that it requires considerable study and application to perform it effectively. It well may be the most difficult of the eighteen to carry off. The exact period of composition is unknown, but it appears to have been written by an older and physically ailing John Field. Without the inclusion of motif #4 in brilliant runs of 32nd notes, and a fluid, active accompaniment, Number Fifteen remains earthbound and very like a lament.

However, if the interpreter gives everything that Field asks for in the score, the audience will experience all the emotion that reasonably well-adjusted concertgoers can absorb in five minutes.

CHAPTER TWENTY:

NOCTURNE NO. 16

At first hearing, I had negative feelings about this Nocturne. Apparently going everywhere and nowhere, it seemed to lack a center, nor was it telling a coherent story. Upon reflection, this was not a surprising reaction, because Number Sixteen, at 172 bars, is the longest of the eighteen by a considerable margin.

There is an odd mix of elements here, even for a John Field Nocturne: passages of crystalline delicacy that anticipate Chopin at his most enchanting, and passages of brooding darkness and pain that cast the long shadow of Beethoven. At the same time, these disparate moods take the stage episodically, with little if any relationship one to the other.

Yes, contrast and ambivalence are intrinsic to Field's music, but in Number Sixteen I could discover no center toward which and from which the story progressed. I concluded that it was an ambitious failure.

But repeated hearings and analysis revealed that there is, after all, a unifying thread, a story. The wandering, episodic character is precisely what Field was striving for. These 172 bars are a memoir, a summing up, rather than a single story or chapter of a larger work. Biographical information supports this interpretation. The piece was written in 1835 when Field was returning to Russia by train. He had barely survived a serious illness while in Italy, and had been rescued by his Russian friends. At that moment it would be fitting for him to be exploring the heights and depths of his experiences, and once again acknowledging his debt to Beethoven.

The connecting link is the modest theme that first appears in bar 9. It rises stepwise from E to A and then falls back a step, a weary yearning phrase, a pale version of those that we encountered in the early Nocturnes. This figure is repeated, with minor variations, throughout. If it does not suggest that the poet is spent, he seems at least resigned.

The many contrasts, nuances and rapid changes of mood in this episodic Nocturne present a major interpretive challenge. In common with Number Ten, which was equally Introspective and Idyllic by turns, no single tempo will serve. Marked Molto Moderato, with a MM quarter note=88, we are headed for disaster. Played at that tempo, Number Sixteen will sound like a hyperactive music box. I perform most of the passages at MM quarter note=63, but increase the tempo for certain passages that I will later identify.

In keeping with its length, Number Sixteen begins with an eight-bar introduction that forecasts the principal motif and also returns in bar 79 to provide a link between two contrasting sections. These eight bars inform us that we should not expect a soothing or comforting experience. The key is C, but the introduction begins in G, and in bar 1 we find a C-sharp, an edgy chromatic that is foreign to both keys. In bar 3, a B-flat7, another alien, nudges the G7 aside. When we finally reach the repeated tonic C in bar 4, we are not home yet. Before reaching the tonic chord in bar 6, the melodic line must pass through A7 with a diminished 5th, and G7.

While the C repeats insistently in the remaining three bars of the introduction, our emotions will continue to be roiled. In bar 6, an E-flat diminished chord imposes itself *sforzando* on the tonic. After a two-beat respite, a more gentle F diminished appears for two beats and then resolves into the tonic. In this brief span we have several motif #8, plus one each of motifs #1, 2 and 3.

During this masterful introduction, which recalls a tactic that Beethoven often used, Field seems to be telling us that we are going to have some unsettling experiences, but we will never be far from home, i.e., who we are.

The first twenty-two bars of the main theme present a lovely mix of the Introspective and Idyllic styles. There are no accents, no sudden outbursts, no impassioned struggle. The modest crescendos provide a gentle emotional pulse to the yearning phrases. The 32nd notes are an elaborate ornamentation, rather than a determined flight to the upper regions. After the brief flight that ends in bar 15, those charming sixths float downward, conclude with a sigh going into bar 17, and are followed by a sequence of five nostalgic, yearning phrases.

This retelling of the familiar story is all about the joy of singing, Field reassures us, and demonstrates by reaching up to the E above high C, first with the sixths and then, in bar 23, with the sequence of triplets that descend with such grace and ease. The song is his reward and consolation, and the object of his struggle, a truth that he stresses with the three-note phrases in bars 25 and 26 that begin on an accented G and peak on high C. That G is repeated emphatically on the first two beats of bars 25-27 and requires the added emphasis of a *sostenuto*.

This is followed by what strikes me as one of the most playful passages in all of the Nocturnes. This child-like, carefree skipping about is totally new and unexpected. It is also just like Field to abruptly stop the fun with four ominous chords and a thunderous *sforzando* in bar 33.

If this Nocturne actually is a summing up, there are two possible explanations for the passage beginning at bar 33. The most obvious is that it depicts the extremes in Field's emotional life, the days—perhaps only hours— of joy interrupted by a disappointment, a psychic blow, even a period of inexplicable depression and despair. This bi-polar existence is already a familiar story, related in almost every Nocturne. Another explanation is that Field probably understood that, because of his fragile and deteriorating health, he was approaching the end of his life, and he had a need to acknowledge his profound debt to Beethoven. He did this in his Nocturne Number Nine, but he may have felt a need to make it part of his memoir Nocturne.

Besides the Opus 27 No. 2 of Beethoven, one of the sonatas that seized Field's imagination and provided him with much of his musical language was the Opus 12 (Pathetique). If you have the score, check the slow introduction to the first movement. It begins with four yearning phrases, motif #1, sighs, motif #2, several outbursts, motif #3, a flight of 32nd notes, motif #4, frequent change of mode from minor to major, motif #6, a struggle, motif #7, and thrusting accented notes, and minor and major seconds, motif #8.

However, this is not the passage that Field is quoting in Nocturne Sixteen. In the second movement, Adagio Cantabile, a secondary theme begins *dolente* in bar 37. A plaintive melody sings above triplets in the inner voices. On the sixth bar of this passage the theme takes on a new life with powerful *sforzando* chords in treble and bass, and then a bar marked *brillante* and *fortissimo*. But this story is not progressing as we were led to expect. The theme abruptly drops two octaves from its highest point, lands *forte*, and then ebbs like a wave that has just crashed against a sea wall. The melody and the inner triplets return, *tranquillo*.

In his Nocturne, Field follows this crashing and ebbing with a cadenza, a sad, lone voice, ad lib. This is modeled after the final bar of the introduction described above, and bar 22 of the second movement. The melody accompanied by inner voices is delayed but eventually appears in the Nocturne at bar 42 and concludes at bar 49. There are other interesting parallels:

Beethoven: extended melodic passages are suddenly interrupted by a *fortissimo* chord, twice, followed by a calm passage marked *dolce*.

Field: bars 42-50, melody accompanied by inner voices suddenly interrupted by *sforzando* chords four times, followed by calm and serenity.

Beethoven: triplets accented on the first note progressing downward, motif #2.

Field: bars 57-58, a series of accented triplets descending, motif #2.

Most important of all, the emotional tone and aura of the Beethoven Adagio and this Nocturne, from bars 32-53, are almost identical. The heart of the matter is that if the interpreter is seeking the essential John Field, he must first make his way through Beethoven. Field acquired from the Master not only his musical language but the courage to express his deepest, most personal emotions.

Musicologists are in agreement about the influence of the cantilena on Field's style. The cantilena is a cradlesong, but the term also refers to a style of soothing vocal music. This is obviously present in most of the Nocturnes, but Field was also strongly influenced by operatic music of a much more dramatic nature. In the aria, the soloist has a degree of expressive freedom because the song is also part of the dramatic action, and the orchestra is obliged to follow and support the soloist. In these Nocturnes there are numerous examples of the upper voice taking on the role of the operatic singer. One interesting and probably controversial example occurs in bar 31 of number Sixteen.

In all of the recordings of this Nocturne, bar 31 is played in strict time. My sense of this music tells me that such an approach robs this moment of its meaning. In fact, from bar 28, the frolicking two-note phrases should be delivered in the style of a coloratura soprano who is coquettishly playing with the notes. In bar 31 the rhythm should be especially relaxed as the singer reaches up for the highest notes. This interpretation is supported by the deliberate slowing of the movement in bar 32 just before the crashing *sforzando*. In this manner, the music becomes portentous and more dramatic.

The *a capriccio* passage, beginning at bar 35, is also operatic in style and should be played *molto espressivo* for maximum effect. I suggest that bars 36 and 37 be performed in this same style, with a return to *a tempo* in bar 38. It is as though Field needs this moment in his memoir to unburden himself. The rest of the story can wait until he has his say, until he can reveal the full extent of his unacknowledged debt to Beethoven. This will require sixteen more bars, from the *a tempo* through bar 53. During those sixteen bars, the upper voice should sing out, especially in bars 47-49; and the *sforzando* in bars 50-52 should explode on impact with a passion that would please the Master himself.

This is followed by a fervent six-bar duet that pleads to be performed with operatic expressiveness. And then the coloratura returns, bars 60-63, with a stunning display of agility and charm that leads us to another place, another mood.

The passage beginning at bar 64 and ending at bar 78 is a motif #5. Marked *dolce,* and graced by numerous sixths, it is a blissful interlude, a needed relief from the emotional turbulence and unpredictability of the preceding section. To support this lighter mood, a slightly quicker tempo, circa MM quarter note=72-76, would be appropriate. A *rallentando* at bar 78 will bring the story back to the introductory theme and MM quarter note=69.

In bar 72 the *diminuendo* that begins *piano* is misplaced. If obeyed, you would find yourself at triple *piano* when you reach the *sforzando* in bar 76. Move the *diminuendo* to the fourth beat of bar 74. The *sforzanados* are a rude awakening from the lovely interlude, and they should be struck for full effect.

The passage from bars 90 to 108 requires a slower tempo for full expression, but not as slow as the principal theme. Try a *ritardando* at bar 88 and post a Meno Mosso MM quarter note=66 at the third beat of bar 89.

In bars 89-90, we have another operatic moment. Do not play those 16ths in strict time but rather expressively, *sostenuto.* The passage that follows, bars 91-108, is all about Field's ambivalence, the pull between opposite emotional poles. In bar 91, the 16ths are flirting with high C until the *sforzando* chord in bar 92 pulls them down in a series of four-note sighs. A variant of this motif begins in bar 95, where the joyful trill and 32nd notes are repeated in a sequence that falters and sinks an octave-and-a-half. This section is completed by two additional variants of the rising and falling motif. In the same operatic spirit, employ *sostenuto* in bar 101 where the singer reaches for that heavily accented high C. Play this eighteen-bar passage with a flexible rhythm that allows the contrasting emotions full expression.

With bar 109, Beethoven returns in a nine-bar passage that requires an *agitato* to be posted at the start. Along with a quicker tempo, quarter note=72, there should be a constant rise and fall of sonority, not all of which are indicated in this edition. In bar 113, drop to *piano* on the last beat and begin another crescendo to the *forte* in bar 115. In bar 117 a *poco rit.* will bring you back to *a tempo* in bar 118.

At this point we have an eight-bar passage that picks up the bi-polar subtheme. In bars 118-122 a sequence of repetitive phrases in 16ths ends on a note two steps higher than the starting note. This is followed by a sequence of triplets in which the starting note is a step-and-a-half higher than the final note. The second triplet in each set is also a sigh. The passage ends in a duet sigh in bar 126.

With the return of the principal theme in bar 126, we have a repetition modified by several improvisational changes (bars 130-138). Then, instead of plunging back into the Pathetique once again, there is a short transition to one of the loveliest and most lilting passages in all the Nocturnes. Here Field expresses the pure joy of singing and gratitude for the gift of song. The entire last section, from bar 126 to the *smorzando*, bar 170, can be played effectively at the tempo of the principal theme.

The triplet 16ths beginning at bar 158 are unexpected, yet appropriate as a way of endowing the song with a spiritual quality, and affirming that the struggle is worth the cost. For three bars, the slowly rising triplets are accompanied by that comforting lower voice. Then three voices below the triplet form an F minor triad with an accented dominant C that becomes the tonic when the chord is resolved in the next bar. As the triplets continue rising to an octave above high C, the F minor-to-C major cadence is repeated.

This episode is pure Beethoven, almost a benediction, recalling the close of the first movement of the Master's fourth concerto, and passages in his fifth concerto. If Field could not bring himself to dedicate one of his compositions to Beethoven, as Schubert did, he could at least give him the honor of closing his memoir Nocturne.

Before we take leave for the next Nocturne, several technical matters require attention. Some lengthy passages have no pedal marks where pedal is obviously a necessity. The eight-bar introduction is too bare and austere without pedal. To avoid excessive resonance, try pedaling on beats 1, 2 and 4 in bars 1 and 2, and on beats 1 and 3 in bars 4-7. In bars such as 10 and 11, where the bass figure continues moving forward, another pedal on the third beat is called for. There are passages, such as bars 40-44, where pedal ought to be applied with each change of harmony. In bars 46-53, pedal on beats 1 and 3. At bar 54, pedal can be eliminated for the purpose of creating a different color, appropriate to the sudden change in style. In bars 64-79, pedal should be changed on beat 3, rather than extended for the entire bar. The passages marked *dolce* also require a lightening of resonance. In those bars with chromatics and rapid changes of harmony in the treble, retaining the single pedal tends to muddy the effect.

Regarding matters of performance, there are several points to be made. In every instance where there are 16th or 32nd notes rising in a crescendo, consider some degree of *sostenuto*. This is particularly recommended in bars 12 and 14. Another example, involving 16ths, is in bars 19-20.

Single accented notes in these Nocturnes often require the added emphasis of a slight *sostenuto*. Examples are in bars 4, 25, 26, 57, 58 and 61.

Some matters involve amending the score. In bar 16 there is no indication of where the crescendo will peak. And in bar 17, the *piano* is misplaced. That dominant chord on the first beat should be marked *mezzo forte,* the peak of the crescendo, and the *piano* moved to the beginning of the next phrase, a motif #1.

The crescendo beginning in bar 36 apparently goes on and on as far as bar 53, with its blessed *diminuendo*. Instead, let it peak at *forte* in bar 38 and diminish in bar 42 to a *mezzo forte* on the fourth beat. Let it diminish further in bar 45 and become *piano* in the next bar. When the *sforzandos* break the calm in bar 50, bring the dynamic up to *mezzo forte*, and diminish in bar 53, as indicated. A *diminuendo* is missing in bar 58, and *piano* should be entered on the first beat of bar 59.

After those lovely sixths in bars 64-67, the melody is formed in thirds. When the alto voice performs counterpoint in bars 69 and 70, it should stay lower and allow the melody to stand out. This is not a true duet in the sense that the two upper voices are equal.

Another passage that would benefit by the vocal style starts on the fourth beat of bar 89. In the recordings I have heard, invariably this is played in strict time, a style that trivializes the passage. Build the crescendo with some deliberation, and a *sostenuto* starting on the way down. This run in 16ths leads to another section in which the song goes bi-polar, with phrases buoyantly rising, followed by phrases drooping. After the *sforzando* in bar 92, a slight *sostenuto* on the first two beats will assist the contrast. This applies to bars 93 and 94 as well. Experiment with a *sostenuto* on the ascent and descent of passages with pronounced crescendos, as in bars 101-102, 103-104 and 105-106. These can also be interpreted as elaborate, two-bar variants of motif #1.

Dynamics are missing in bars 113-114. A *piano* should be posted on the fourth beat of bar 113, and another crescendo should begin on the second beat of the next bar. The score indicates that bars 135-139 are to be played *piano,* but there are genuine opportunities for expression. Try a crescendo on the first beat of bar 136, but instead of peaking with a *mezzo forte* on the high F, play it *subito piano* and descend gracefully. You could start another crescendo on the fourth beat of bar 137 and peak *mezzo forte* on the accented G in the next bar. Then begin *piano* again on the third beat of bar 139. The *diminuendo* is missing in bar 140.

There is ample opportunity in this Nocturne to find your own voice while discovering that of John Field. Experiment until you are satisfied that you are telling the story in as compelling a manner as you can. In the process, you will probably have an experience similar to my own: every time you go back to Number Sixteen you will find something new.

CHAPTER TWENTY-ONE:

NOCTURNE NO. 17

This is the second of the Nocturnes that are not a Nocturne by even the broadest possible definition of the term. Infused with sunlight, activity and a dose of mischief, this piece should have been titled "Scherzo."

One cannot imagine Field composing a more lighthearted piece than this. Constantly surprising us with unexpected harmonies, changes of tempo, and syncopations, it is infectious. The editing is the best of the lot. The tempo of MM quarter note=80 is just right, and the absence of pedal in all but eight of the 78 bars is also close to perfect. This piece requires a bright, uncluttered sound that allows the accents and staccatos to snap. In fact, the indicated pedaling adds nothing and could be eliminated.

Although some of the introspective motifs appear, their function is totally altered by the atmosphere of this playful music. As demonstrated here, the motifs alone do not create a nocturne unless they are in the right context and their motives are pure.

The Peters edition calls for MM quarter note=60. This considerably slower tempo evidently is an attempt to evoke whatever nocturnal qualities Number Seventeen might possess. This tempo does linger over the occasional minor chord and the passing notes that form major and minor seconds. With the use of pedal, the accented notes acquire more thrust. Some of the descending two-note phrases more closely resemble sighs. The effect is that of someone smiling through his tears.

On the negative side, there are several figures, such as rising 16ths and dotted 16ths and accented or staccato notes that are so innately energetic, they demand an appropriate tempo. The worst moment occurs in bars 56-58, where every beat is a quarter note. The effect is funereal. However, I recommend that the reader play Number Seventeen at this tempo and discover whether or not it has sufficient emotional pull to win you over.

This disparity between the editions is further evidence of the serious problem that contemporary pianists face when trying to present a satisfying and revelatory performance of these Nocturnes. There has been so much tampering with the texts, no one—at least at the present time—can assure us of what is authentic John Field. All of the concert pianists with whom I have had a dialogue tell me that they consult a variety of editions and sources in shaping their interpretations. Not one depends on a single edition.

Although Number Seventeen does not belong in a collection of Nocturnes, it deserves to be performed. Only moderately difficult, it would brighten up any student recital.

CHAPTER TWENTY-TWO:

NOCTURNE NO. 18

The last of the eighteen Nocturnes shares with number Seven and number Ten the distinction of having been written originally for piano and string quartet. All three also begin with an introduction for strings, with one major difference. The introductory section of number Eighteen is only sixteen bars long and is included in all of the editions as an integral part of the Nocturne.

This music may have worked reasonably well as a piano quintet, but as a piano solo it presents challenging interpretive problems. No pianist can possibly make musical sense of this work unless it is performed in a variety of tempi. The objection to such an approach that might have been raised with regard to Nocturne Seven can also be raised here. And the solution is the same. A recording of Divertissment No. 2 by the same artists reveals that the strings again fade nearly to obscurity when the piano enters, and simply follow the pianist's lead. The recorded rendition, however, is quite inadequate. The tempo of the entire piece is much too slow, and the Cantando section drags pitiably. This tempo may have been chosen in order to accommodate bars 30 and 31, which become pure gibberish when performed too quickly. Starting the Cantando at a reasonable tempo and playing the two bars *espressivo e molto sostenuto* would have solved the problem. The *scherzando* section is also desecrated by taking it at a tempo that is much too rapid and totally out of character with this Nocturne.

The MM quarter note=72 is about right for the introduction. But after a *ritardando* and a double bar, the main section of the Nocturne is introduced with Cantando (in a singing style) posted at the head. It is as though the curtain has gone up and the soprano takes the stage. Unfortunately, the tempo suitable for the instrumental introduction will not serve the singer.

Further, there are passages in which the song stops and the music becomes contemplative and somewhat melancholy. Articulated mostly in quarter notes, these passages sound elegiac and present an excessively stark contrast to the melodic section. Consequently, the urge to hasten the tempo appropriately should not be resisted. The *scherzando* passage clearly calls for a faster tempo, as does the *piu agitato* later on. Unlike number Ten, this final Nocturne does not have an improvisational character; each passage is rather like a set piece in a miniature drama.

After much thought and experimentation, I concluded that number Eighteen would best be treated as an Adagio, in the manner of the slow movements of Beethoven's late piano sonatas, with their frequent changes of mood and tempo. Just as a point of reference and a general guide, I offer the following MM settings.

The introduction: quarter note=69. The Cantando, which ends at bar 36, quarter note=56. The *scherzando,* bars 57-64, quarter note=80. Bars 65-78, quarter note=69. The *piu agitato,* bars 79-83, quarter note=72. Bars 84-87, quarter note=60. Bars 88-92, quarter note=56. Finish with a *rallentando.*

Within this framework, a piece of music that would strike one as episodic and disjointed at a faster tempo becomes coherent and quite affecting. The poet's story is about a brave attempt to continue his song and reach for the heights despite recurring periods of melancholy and despair. This may not appear to be substantially different from the earlier stories, but here we have only one brief period of struggle, and a single flight to D above high C. The poet is essentially earthbound; every movement upward is followed by a sinking toward middle C. Sadly, the attempt to elevate his spirits in the *scherzando* passage is brief. After eight bars he is back to his brooding.

If this story is not appealing, the pianist can develop another by raising all of the suggested tempi two or three notches and lifting the mood. Since all ten introspective motifs are here in abundance, there are numerous opportunities for emotive expression.

At whatever tempo this Nocturne is performed, the melody must be sung out, and the rhythm allowed the flexibility to release the soul of the music. The lovely melody, accompanied by the comforting flow of broken triads, begins with a motif #1 that spans two bars. This is followed by a shorter version, like a consoling comment. In bars 20-21, a slightly altered version of the first phrase rises to its apex with a *ritardando* rather than a crescendo. This stresses the highly expressive character not only of the melody but of the entire piece.

At this point, I believe that it would be illuminating to consider the numerous parallels between this Nocturne and the Largo of Beethoven's Opus 10 No. 3. Although one is marked Molto Moderato, and the other Largo, the actual performance tempo of the Cantando section is Adagio, and both pieces find their fullest expression when played slowly.

In the Largo we find an eight-bar introduction that establishes the mood, complete with yearning phrases, sighs and an expansive melody in the upper register, just below high C. The Nocturne has a sixteen-bar introduction. In both pieces, the melody contains embellishments in 16th and 32nd notes. In both there are leaping notes, *forte* and accented, and rapid descents to *piano*. In both there are sudden and unexpected *sforzandos*, followed by calm. The Largo has a second subject, thirteen bars long, marked *animato un pochettino*. The Nocturne has a *scherzando* section eight bars long. The Largo contains several chords with unresolved passing tones, played *fortissimo*. In bars 77 and 81 of the Nocturne we find a B-flat diminished with an added F that anticipates the F in bar 78. In bar 81, the D-flat diminished, *forte* and accented, includes A-flat, which becomes the tonic of the A-flat chord in bar 82. And finally, the emotional aura of both pieces is similar.

Mr. Piggott informs us that number Eighteen is the only Nocturne actually to be published as a quintet. The version in this edition is an exact replica of the piano part. Mr. Piggott also states that the principal melody is ". . . very Italianate in character, which might be a romance sung by a heroine from some Bellini opera." Quite so. But he is also dismissive of number Eighteen, despite its lovely melody, describing it as undistinguished and unpianistic.

This appraisal is not justified. Granted, this last Nocturne does not have the brilliant passages and dramatic moments of several others; but when performed at its full dynamic range, it evokes genuine emotion with its changing moods, expressive melody, and lovely harmonic sequences. To maximize your chances for success, I repeat my mantra: come to this piece through Beethoven and his Adagios.

Before moving on, there are some matters of interpretation that require special attention.

In bar 31, no attempt should be made to play those descending two-note phrases in strict time, even at the slower tempo. Just allow them to float downward at will. They are miniature motif #2 phrases, and rushing merely robs them of any expressive content. Neither should you play the run of 32nd notes, bar 35, in strict tempo.

After that climactic and triumphant *sforzando* in bar 36, pause before proceeding to the contemplative passage marked *dolce*. A *fermata* should have been placed over the bar line, and its omission, either by Field or his editors, was evidently determined by their desire to publish the score in its original form. However, as a piano solo that carries the full emotional freight of the music, some changes are necessary.

If you prefer to lighten the mood and attend to the *dolce* in bar 37, don't hesitate to move the tempo along a bit. All that matters is the total effect.

The *scherzando* passage should be livelier, but not so fast that it is totally out of character with the rest of the Nocturne. Only your ear and intuition will guide you. As a point of reference, I usually perform this passage at MM quarter note=72.

When playing those broken octaves in bars 51, 84 and 86, the lower F should be struck exactly on the beat with the F in the bass.

The concluding passage calls for a ten-bar *ritardando,* beginning at bar 87. This is not possible. Neither the Peters nor the Kalmus editions offers a viable alternative, both instructing the baffled pianist to keep retarding until the end. No pianist with any sense will pay the slightest attention. After the *ritardando* in bar 87, I post a Piu Lento and maintain the slower tempo until bar 93, where I begin a final *rallentando.*

As expected, the pedal marks are scarce and inconsistent. The second bar with its *sforzando* should be pedaled, as it is in bar 10. Also pedal bar 6. The Cantando section, from bar 17 to 36, requires a sonority enhanced by the pedal. In almost every bar, except where your ear guides you differently, a pedal on each beat would be appropriate. Bars 31 and 32 should not be pedaled. The *scherzando* passage with its detached chords, *pianissimo*, is much more effective without pedal until the *sforzando* at bar 63.

This Nocturne is the voice of a poet whose passions are more temperate, and who has reached a place of acceptance, perhaps resignation. He achieves a balance between longing and joy, and blends a surface simplicity with the ever-shifting flow of emotion. From the lovely melodic line to the passing stings of colliding harmonies, Nocturne Eighteen is a touching poem and a summing up of the essential John Field.

CHAPTER TWENTY-THREE:

THE ENIGMATIC GENIUS

The word "enigmatic" was chosen with care. We know quite a bit about the exterior life of John Field. Musicologists have traced his travels and public appearances from Dublin, his place of birth, to London, to many of the major cities of Europe, to Russia, France, Italy, and finally back to Moscow, where he died. But we know almost nothing about the private man, the thinking and feeling John Field.

We have only half a dozen letters in his hand, none of which provides any insight into his private world. Apparently he confided in no one. None of his friends, associates, students or contemporaries who wrote biographies or memoirs included a scrap of intimate information, insight or revelation. Written in Russian, German and French, these books were translated or read in the original language by Patrick Piggott, who has nothing pertinent to report on our subject.

The contemporary world observed Field's demeanor on stage, his public behavior, his unconventional dress, his indifference to social norms and niceties, his apparent unconcern about the fate of his music. To this day, our only analytical portrait of Field the man comes to us by way of the Franz Liszt essay, which was discussed at some length in Chapter Two. There is no need to review that material here, since there is compelling evidence that all of it was based on a superficial knowledge of Field, or fabricated for reasons about which we can only speculate.

I cannot think of another musical figure of importance, from Bach forward, who remains so enigmatic. Of course, we know considerably more about some than others. Mozart, for example, wrote numerous letters to his father that reveal his thoughts and feelings on matters musical and otherwise. In his own words and in the testimony of his contemporaries, we know a great deal about Beethoven's passion and despair, and thoughts about a wide variety of subjects. The emotional and psychological struggles of Schubert, Schumann and Chopin make them three-dimensional characters. In the instance of Gustav Mahler, every step in his career, every nuance in his spiritual and emotional life was shared with friends, recorded in hundreds of letters, and confided to his wife, Alma.

But Field had no Alma, no soul mate in whom he could safely and unconditionally confide. This huge gap in our knowledge has a direct impact on the central concern of this book: how are we to understand and interpret Field's finest compositions, the Nocturnes? In my analysis of each Nocturne, I was compelled to invent an overarching story as a device for entering into the spirit of the music. With no evidence external to the Nocturnes themselves that my conclusions have any validity, I have been left with no other choice than to find that evidence inside the Nocturnes, as well as in the music to which Field was exposed since his early years.

My purpose here is to explore several facets of this enigmatic man and, by coming up with some plausible explanations, circle back to our primary concern, the music. The order in which I address these questions has nothing to do with their relative importance.

The first question: why did Field never reveal the process by which he created, or invented, the short lyrical piece he eventually called Nocturne?

These pieces were so popular, they contributed to and were intimately linked with his hugely successful career as a concert pianist. It is inconceivable that not one of his contemporaries, let alone dozens, asked him that question. Yet we have no record of an explanation. We must wonder, then, how did he respond? Did he say, "I had difficulty sleeping one night, and I arose from my bed, went to the piano, and as my fingers wandered over the keys, as in a dream, this lovely melody came into being. I immediately wrote it down, just as I heard it." That at least would have given us a clue. Or did he say, "I was in a deep sleep one night, and I saw myself in my dream, walking with the loveliest of women beside a lake in the moonlight. And as we gazed into each other's eyes, I could hear strains of music such as I had never heard before. It was so extraordinary, I woke myself up, went to the piano, and played what I had heard in my dream."

Either story would have fully satisfied the inquirer because they confirm the popular conception of creative genius and inspiration. Even professional musicians who have spent nearly a lifetime studying the great composers and their music may subscribe to the magical theory of creativity. For example, in my correspondence with Miceal O'Rourke, who has recorded the complete Nocturnes of Field, I learned that the Nocturne came "out of the blue."

Yet we have no record that the question was asked or answered.

We know, from the testimony of creative people in all the arts, that much of their work is a collaboration between the intellect and the unconscious. The latter functions by absorbing and processing a wide range of experience, which then becomes available to the creative artist. What has not been taken in is not there. Nothing comes from outer space.

For reasons about which we can only speculate, Field did not want to reveal his secret. However, there is a key that may unlock this mystery. The key is Field's own declaration that he never taught his students the music of Haydn, Mozart or Beethoven. This fact is mentioned in Patrick Piggott's *John Field and His Music*, specifically the chapter on Field as a teacher. In addition to his own compositions, he taught the piano music of minor contemporaries of Mozart and Haydn, most of whom are virtually forgotten today.

This revelation by Field is not only curious, it is astounding. Haydn, Mozart and Beethoven were the foremost composers of their day, noted for their piano compositions as well as orchestral works. There is no question that Field had an intimate knowledge of their piano music. Pietro Spada, a concert pianist and musicologist who has recorded the complete works of Field, has devoted many years to an exhaustive study of Muzio Clementi, Field's tutor. In answer to my inquiry, Mr. Spada said, "Field should have to be considered in the mitteleuropean classic tradition, although it is obvious that there are influences of the Irish Folklore and country music in his output. His very strong connection with Clementi, who, in my judgment, is clearly part of the Viennese classic period, must, in some way, have trained him in the highest Viennese traditional culture."

Every serious student of the piano is required to learn at least the early Mozart sonatas. The Adagio of Mozart's very first sonata is a work of considerable beauty and expressiveness, and almost every bar contains at least one of the ten introspective motifs. In fact, all ten occur at least once, and the fundamental motifs #1, 2 and 3 occur multiple times. Is it possible to imagine Field's embarrassment if one of his students were to take notice of the similarities between the Adagio and Field's Nocturnes? Indeed, yes. He avoided the problem by keeping Mozart hidden in the closet.

Some of Field's students were exceptionally talented and performed solo concerts of rather difficult music. A natural and essential part of their training would have included at least the first fifteen Beethoven sonatas, all of which were written and published before Field's twentieth birthday. His failure to include this repertoire cannot be based on a statement that he is reported to have made about not much caring for the piano music of Beethoven. This is pure bluff, a screen behind which he concealed his immense debt to Beethoven; and he had no intention of allowing his students or anyone else to take a good look behind that screen.

A corollary to this question: Why was Field so determined to conceal the sources of his acclaimed creation, the Nocturne? I believe the answer is inseparable from the concept of "image," which is so prominent in our time as it relates to public figures. Music was Field's life, all that really mattered. His achievements as pianist and composer not only brought him acclaim and admiration, they were the source of the income that supported his life of luxury and self-indulgence. Being known as the creator of a new musical form contributed to his mystique, and his income.

It is interesting to compare Field's behavior with that of Schubert. The latter, who could not earn a living as a concert pianist, and who struggled with poverty, always avowed his profound debt to Beethoven. He dedicated a set of variations to Beethoven, and expressed a desire to be buried beside him. Schubert, poor sweet soul, had nothing to hide or protect.

The second question: How can we explain the striking disparity between the public John Field and the pianist/composer?

Numerous reports from a variety of sources confirm that Field was meticulous about every detail in his compositions. Examples: to insure that the pianist produced the proper tone for each note, he provided the fingering for all his piano music. Even after publication, some of his compositions were subjected to correction and alteration until the last year of his life. He resisted allowing publication of one of his Nocturnes until late in his life, and then only after the insistent urging of friends.

In public, Field was frequently seen inebriated. His dress was eccentric and carelessly assembled. At social events and parties his behavior was sometimes coarse and rude. At one formal dinner, he removed his shoes, apparently because they were uncomfortable. There are reports that he spent days in idleness, smoking cigars and drinking with friends. When given a commission to compose a work for a specific occasion, he tended to delay the task until almost the last moment, when he succumbed to the pressure of his concerned friends.

This is the same man who spent four or five hours daily in grueling exercise at the piano in order to maintain his acclaimed technique. This self-discipline extended to the concert hall, where he often performed flawlessly while under the influence of alcohol.

History is rich in stories about geniuses who were brilliant in their fields but eccentric and surprisingly inept in other areas of their life. Albert Einstein is the most prominent example in modern history. But there are essentially two kinds of eccentricity. One results from absentmindedness or simple unconcern about the ordinary business of daily life. The other kind is a deliberate flaunting and disregard of convention.

It appears that Field was a combination of the two. As a practitioner of the first type, he was genuinely forgetful about prosaic matters. His fees from performing and teaching were sometimes found scattered about the house in odd places, instead of being banked. On at least one occasion he forgot to appear for a concert performance and a search party was sent to find him while the audience waited.

We can understand his motivation for deliberately behaving unconventionally by viewing this behavior within the context of his formative years. As a very young child, he began studies at the piano under the direction of his father and grandfather, both musicians. The training was so rigorous—including physical punishment—that it would be considered child abuse today. The child showed unusual talent, and the father apparently was so determined to produce a prodigy, he moved the family from Dublin to London, where the opportunities and attention would be much greater. There young Field performed to critical acclaim, especially because his publicized age of eight was two years younger than his actual age. He came to the attention of Clementi, who agreed to tutor the lad and advance his career. While studying with Clementi, Field traveled across Europe, paying for his lessons by performing in public on Clementi's invention, an improved piano, which he was selling everywhere. In return for the lessons, Clementi exploited the boy, kept him impoverished, and treated him as a servant.

If we look at these events, spanning a period of some fifteen years, from Field's point of view, we can readily understand why he might be filled with resentment. During his entire childhood and youth, he was under the total control of others, who used him for their own purposes. His father uprooted him from his childhood home and turned him over to a stranger for the remainder of his adolescence. It is my contention that when Field finally established himself and was financially independent, he over-reacted to those years of deprivation and abuse. He simply refused to conform to the expectations of others. He also created a public John Field, a façade, and trusted no one, confided in no one, revealed himself to no one.

Mr. Piggott relates that when Field was in Paris, he informed an Abbe that his father was French, that his name was Duchamp, that he played the violin, and moved to England where he changed his name to Field—almost all of it a fiction. His father did play the violin. He also said that the beatings he received as a child caused him to run away from home for a brief time, but there is no corroborating evidence that this ever happened. Field may have wanted to dramatize his life, or elicit sympathy. The point is that he learned rather early to create a fiction that he presented as John Field.

The relevance of all this, once again, is the music. The performance and creation of music were Field's life. They were the only things that mattered and the only things he could trust. The inner life that he kept from others went into his compositions, particularly the Nocturnes. Thus, we complete the circle. If this analysis is correct, if we are dealing with a bruised, sensitive and insecure human being, then my approach to the Nocturnes is justified. As a true romantic, Field saw no separation between his psyche and his music—and neither should we.

The third question: Why did John Field stop evolving as a composer before the age of forty?

This is the most intriguing question of the three, and probably the most difficult to answer. One could say that Field did evolve. Look at the distance he traveled from the early sonatas to his best Nocturnes. One might argue that, for a minor composer, Field evolved as much as he could, and as much as we have a right to expect. After all, he was no Mozart, Haydn, Beethoven, or Schubert.

The key phrase may be "for a minor composer." He did not compose symphonies or operas, but neither did Chopin, who may not stand among the giants but is certainly in the second rank. Part of the Field lexicon is that between 1823 and 1832 he published almost nothing and may not have composed much more than that. The dates of composition for most of his work are not actually known, and usually are probable guesses. But if the years between his early forties and early fifties were not barren, there is no evidence that they nurtured any significant work. During those years he might have raised his art to another level, as the major composers always do.

An inkling of what Field might have accomplished can be found in the "Grand Pastoral," of which the uncut version is in the Peters edition, Nocturne Number Seventeen. There is a short passage, beginning at bar 77, which contains a harmonic-tonal texture that goes beyond romanticism into the twentieth century. We hear blue notes and jazz-ballade chords a la George Shearing. This is followed by four measures of atmospheric coloration that is intrinsic to impressionism. Had Field developed his obvious interest in and talent for chamber music, he might have produced some extraordinary work and secured his place in the second rank.

Contemporary observers agreed that among Field's traits, some of which were charming and attractive, was laziness. With the income from a single concert, he could afford to indulge in uninterrupted socializing for weeks. As the years progressed, he became increasingly averse to composing new music and turned mostly to revising older works and recasting chamber works into solos. As his dependence on alcohol increased, his health began to decline. The answer to my question may be that, under these conditions, Field had just enough left to continue performing, which contemporary reports say remained on a very high level.

But I am not entirely satisfied with that explanation. There are too many examples of composers who created some of their best work while struggling with either serious emotional or health problems, sometimes both. It is possible that Field's problem was the creative process itself. His symbiotic relationship with Beethoven nourished him in the early years of his career; but eventually this worked against him. He had exhausted the short, lyrical form, and was not comfortable with the larger forms. His concertos were two-movement works, into which he inserted an existing nocturne (as in the first movement of Concerto No. 7), or for which he improvised the second movement during the performance. He apparently had no feeling for musical architecture, for the grand design. His music was simply a natural extension of his psyche, a channel for his emotions.

The final, bitter irony is that when Field studied Beethoven's late-period work, he was convinced that the Master had done it all, taken music as far as it could go. Beethoven quite possibly intimidated Field as he did Brahms, who agonized for decades before producing his first symphony.

Throughout the history of music, there are tragic stories of genius cut down at an early age, with the consequent loss to the culture of the world. There is no need to list the well-known names of those who died before the age of forty, or thirty-five. But I find in the life story of John Field another name that could be added to that list. The final flowering of his genius was cut short, not by death, but by a combination of character flaws and circumstance. If Field had died in 1825, little about his career and contribution would have been altered.

The only possible alleviation of that loss is to present to the world his most beautiful and enduring creations, the Nocturnes, as I believe Field meant them to be heard.

CHAPTER TWENTY-FOUR:

FIELD ON DISC

Since the revival of interest in John Field started to build around 1970, several pianists have recorded his entire output, while some have recorded only the Nocturnes. The performances of the sonatas, rondos, variations and fantasias are generally similar. But any knowledgeable person who listens to the renditions of the Nocturnes in close proximity, say over a day or two, must be impressed—perhaps even stunned—by the wide range and diversity of interpretations.

Among these artists, John O'Conor is most closely associated with Field. His recordings of the concertos and Nocturnes are the most frequently aired on my local classical music station. I consider O'Conor to be among the best of an outstanding group of contemporary pianists. His recorded performances of classical masters, such as Beethoven and Schubert, are deeply felt expositions that bring out the full emotional range of the music. His interpretation of Field's music is absolutely charming, full of life and color—until he performs the Nocturnes.

This disconnect between the sonatas, for example, and the Nocturnes is utterly baffling. In a letter to me, O'Conor spoke of his reaction to the Liszt essay on Field: "I find much of it romantically very fanciful. However I like the way he gets to the heart of the essence of Field's style so quickly and doesn't try to inflate the pieces in any way. It is because of their simplicity that they have retained their unique charm."

As a cultural Irish icon, Field is almost universally regarded as a bard in the old Irish tradition. Coming out of this tradition, O'Conor has no difficulty or hesitancy about ignoring the numerous instructions and dynamic marks in the score that make it abundantly clear that these are not charming and simple songs. By flattening the dynamics and eliminating accents, both heavy and light, O'Conor performs all of the Nocturnes as though they are Idyllic. When the Introspective intensity and yearning is eliminated, we are left without the drama, only a lovely song. Any reader still unconvinced that Field ever wrote an Introspective Nocturne, as I have attempted to describe them, will find great pleasure and delight in O'Conor's charming, tender, and loving performances.

Pietro Spada is one of the artists who have recorded all of Field's music for piano solo. The reader may recall that in the preceding chapter, Spada placed Field in the classical Viennese school, along with Mozart, Clementi, Haydn, Beethoven and Schubert. It is no surprise that his performance of Field's music takes into account the considerable dynamic range found in the sonatas, rondos, variations and fantasias. But in the Nocturnes, there is a softening of dynamics—*fortes* usually become *mezzo fortes*—and many of the accents are either blunted or eliminated, especially *sforzandos*.

Despite his sensitive and quite lovely performances, Spada frequently misses opportunities to raise the Nocturnes to a higher level of expressiveness. One example is the *sospirando* passage in the second Nocturne, which Spada performs in strict meter. The *con dolore* in bars 61-62 is not delayed with even the slightest *sostenuto*. In Nocturne Three, the middle section, Piu Moderato, is played at the same tempo as the opening, leaving a deeper level of emotion untouched. Field had a good reason for slowing the tempo of the remainder of this Nocturne; he had a story to tell, but unfortunately, no one is telling it. In Nocturne Seven, the tempo is too fast, the dynamics are muted, and the 32nd notes that practically cry out for *sostenuto e espressivo* are dashed off *a tempo*. *Sforzandos* are frequently missing, and *fortes* are muted.

Happily, Nocturne Eight emerges as a true beauty under Spada's fingers. Although some *fortes* are muted, the phrasing is highly expressive, the rhythm appropriately flexible, and the totality of the performance quite affecting. This is genuine John Field and, for teachers and students, worth the price of the disc.

Generally, however, despite the obvious virtues in Spada's interpretation of the Nocturnes, he must reach another level of expression and intensity before the stories in these pieces are told.

Miceal O'Rourke's recordings also present us with a mixed bag. His performances of the Concertos are excellent, lyrical and brilliant in turn. The full dynamic and emotional range is there. His interpretations of the Nocturnes are improvisational and consequently closer to Field's intent than those of O'Conor and Spada. He appropriately applies *sostenuto* and *rubato*, and shapes the phrase. But in the true Irish tradition, in order to produce a beautiful song, he softens the dynamics and eliminates numerous accents, including *sforzandos*. In Nocturne Number One he ignores the *scherzando* in bar 15, and in the passage from bar 20 to 27, the intense yearning and passion is lost because he softens the *forte* and all the accents, as well as the implied *espressivo*.

O'Rourke is also unpredictable and erratic, sometimes pushing his interpretations into territory far beyond the bounderies of the John Field Nocturne. For example, the third Nocturne begins Un Poco Allegretto. Allegretto is usually in the neighborhood of 112-120 to a beat. Poco Allegretto is around 104-112. O'Rourke begins at MM 8th=126, Allegro, and much too fast. Twenty-eight bars into the piece there is a *ritardando* and the instruction Piu Moderato. There is no ambiguity about what the composer wants. The pianist must slow the tempo, come down from the *allegretto* and perform the next section more moderately. O'Rourke not only ignores this change of tempo and mood, he plays the remainder of the piece at 8th=132, a tempo faster than the opening. The matter of tempo aside, the effect of those galloping triads in the bass is to utterly destroy the nocturnal texture and mood.

This sort of extreme and uncalled for deviation also occurs in other Nocturnes, where the most frequent offense is a too-rapid tempo. My impression is that, while O'Rourke has a genuine emotional connection with the Nocturnes, he is more intent on satisfying his own needs than in exploring the music for Field's voice. He strikes me as lacking the artistic integrity that O'Conor and Spada so amply display. At the same time, when O'Rourke is good, he is very good. If the reader is looking for some fine examples of the improvisational style to which I have frequently referred, listen to O'Rourke's Nocturne album.

The fourth pianist whose work I examined is Hans Kahn. He recorded the complete Nocturnes on the Tuxedo label, a European company that may no longer be in business.

Hope dies hard. I purchased this CD, by a pianist about whom I knew nothing, with the hope that I might stumble upon the ideal interpreter of Field's Nocturnes. Alas and alack! Mr. Kahn is evidently a graduate *cum laude* of the Liszt School of John Field performance. These Nocturnes are as lively and sunny as a spring day after a winter thaw. They are all launched at tempi several notches higher than those of any of the other pianists. If O'Rourke takes Number One at 60, Kahn drives it up to 84, and tosses aside all the dynamics in his gambol through Eden. If O'Rourke takes Number Two at 76, Kahn goes up to 88. In the third Nocturne, Kahn is a little less enthusiastic, or energetic, and takes the Poco Allegretto at 120; but, in common with O'Rourke, plays the Piu Moderato even faster.

I cannot help wishing that Field had posted a Piu Lento instead, which might have prevented this abuse. But he may have deliberately avoided using the term *"lento"* out of fear that the passage would be played too slowly. This is an excellent example of where the posting of a MM by the composer would have been helpful. Field may have done so, but I am unaware of any composition of his in which he assigned a MM.

Of course, the too-rapid tempi taken by Kahn strangle any expression of genuine and affecting emotion in these pieces. And to insure that none of these stories is told, he constantly rushes past dynamic markings without so much as a passing glance or a reflecting pause. This set of recordings possesses no virtue that would induce me to recommend it.

All of the CD's that were investigated are available on the internet from Wherehouse.com and from Amazon.com. Wherehouse stocks both new and used CD's, the latter at extremely low prices. However, if you intend to put the disc to heavy use, I suggest that you purchase it new.

John O'Conor records with the Telarc label. CD-80290 contains the four sonatas and Nocturnes 3, 7 and 17. The sonatas are beautifully performed, true gems, and worth the price of the CD. His superb performance of piano concertos No. 2 and No. 3 are on CD-80370.

Pietro Spada records on the Arts Music label. The complete works are on six discs, referred to as volumes. Volume 4 contains Nocturnes 1-15. The remaining Nocturnes appear in Volume 5, along with the four Fantasias. Played with sensitivity and a delicate, expressive touch, they can be instructive and delightful despite their rhythmic inflexibility and muted dynamics.

Miceal O'Rourke records for the Chandos label. The complete Nocturnes are on disc CHAN8719/20.

The Nocturnes that I gradually discovered over a period of several years are not yet available on disc. But the recordings by O'Conor, Spada and O'Rourke provide an entryway that can be extremely helpful to professionals, amateurs and students who are unacquainted with this music and anxious to expand their knowledge of the Romantic repertoire.

AFTERWORD

Writing this book has been a strange and fascinating journey. After finishing the first draft, I expected to do some polishing and correct a few minor errors. But when I returned to the first Nocturne, it was as though a veil had been lifted, revealing features and nuances that altered my perception of the music. Over a period of months, this process continued and did not stop until I completed three drafts, each of which reflected my growing comprehension.

There were periods of frustration and doubt about ever completing the work in a form that would satisfy me. After all, music is not chemistry or physics. Once you get past the few facts, you enter the realm of mystery, magic, dreams and spirit.

It was spirit that sustained me, spirit coming from my connection to John Field and going out to my unknown readers. Those connections compelled me to enter as deeply as I could into the life of each Nocturne with emotion and intellect working in tandem. I had no intention of stopping until my obligation to Field and my readers was fulfilled.

Now my earnest hope is that a few will have been so inspired by my enthusiasm and advocacy that they will take a journey similar to my own. May delight, passion and commitment carry those few far beyond the making of pretty music.

Ultimately, one of my readers may be a concert pianist, perhaps a gifted student in a conservatory, who will fall under the spell of John Field, accept the challenge, and bring to the music-loving public the authentic Nocturnes. Field deserves no less. Among the leading Romantics, he is second to none for the sheer beauty of his melodies, the freshness and daring of his harmonic invention, and the intensity of emotion in these lyrical pieces.

I am extremely anxious to hear from you. Send your comments, both favorable and otherwise, to my e-mail address: *Ajbrahms@aol.com*. Ideally, a book such as this should initiate a conversation; so I intend to answer every letter. However, I am leery about opening mail from persons unknown, so please include the subject under your return address. "John Field" or "Nocturnes" will do.